GOD'S LITTLE SUNSHINE

THE AMAZING LIFE OF A DISABLED CHILD
(SPECIAL NEEDS) AND THE UNSHAKEABLE
FAITH OF HER CAREGIVERS

GOD'S LITTLE SUNSHINE

"INSPIRATIONAL, HEARTFELT, UPLIFTING"

ANTOINETTE UPCHURCH

Copyright © 2018 by Antoinette Upchurch

This document is geared towards providing exact and reliable information in regards to the topic and issue covered. The publication is sold with the idea that the publisher is not required to render accounting, officially permitted, or otherwise, qualified services. If advice is necessary, legal or professional, a practiced individual in the profession should be ordered.

From a Declaration of Principles which was accepted and approved equally by a Committee of the American Bar Association and a Committee of Publishers and Associations.

In no way is it legal to reproduce, duplicate, or transmit any part of this document in either electronic means or in printed format. Recording of this publication is strictly prohibited and any storage of this document is not allowed unless with written permission from the publisher. All rights reserved.

The information provided herein is stated to be truthful and consistent, in that any liability, in terms of inattention or otherwise, by any usage or abuse of any policies, processes, or directions contained within is the solitary and utter responsibility of the recipient reader. Under no circumstances will any legal responsibility or blame be held against the publisher for any reparation, damages, or monetary loss due to the information herein, either directly or indirectly.

Respective authors own all copyrights not held by the publisher.

The information herein is offered for informational purposes solely, and is universal as so. The presentation of the information is without contract or any type of guarantee assurance.

The trademarks that are used are without any consent, and the publication of the trademark is without permission or backing by the trademark owner. All trademarks and brands within this book are for clarifying purposes only and are the owned by the owners themselves, not affiliated with this document.

All Scripture quotation, unless otherwise indicated, are taken from the Holy Bible, New International Version®. NIV®. Copyright© 1973, 1978, 1984 by International Bible Society. Used by permission of Zondervan Publishing House.

ISBN: 978-1-943409-39-6

All rights reserved.

DEDICATED

To My Wonderful Granddaughter (Kaiden E. Upchurch)
The Most Amazing, Resilient Human Being I know
She Has A Warrior Spirit and She Is A Fighter
She Has Inspired Me To Never Give Up
She Is God's Little Sunshine

FOREWORD

"God's Little Sunshine" is a book that has been birthed out of pain, hurt, loneliness, depression, defeat, healing, encouragement, miracles and the greatest of all, LOVE. The author, Antoinette Upchurch, experienced every one of these emotions with her precious, angelic granddaughter, Kaiden.

I have had the pleasure of knowing Antoinette for numerous years. She is a woman of extraordinary faith. This faith caused her to believe God when the doctors said Kaiden would never live beyond eight years old. The medical aspect was extremely bleak, but this woman believed and held fast to a hope in a higher power than medical science could give her.

Antoinette's heart of gold, her compassion, is seen in the writing of this book. This book was lived out day by day in her home. This wide-eye, beautiful smiling face caused the entire Upchurch family to love deeply, unconditionally, and see God's miraculous hand in this beautiful little face.

I am so proud to call Antoinette my daughter in the Lord and my friend in Christ Jesus. Thank you for showing all of us how to love beyond measure and to believe in the impossible.

—Gail Dickens

AUTHOR'S ACKNOWLEDGEMENTS

THERE ARE MANY PEOPLE in my life that have contributed to my book in their own ways. I want to give acknowledgements to them. I first would like to acknowledge God and thank him for this opportunity to share my story. The second acknowledgements is to my granddaughters parents Ulyess Upchurch Jr and Velvet McClurkin. I am thankful that these two wonderful people shared their daughter with me and allowed her to be a big part of her life. I will forever be grateful to you all. The third acknowledgment is to Ulysses Upchurch, my husband; thanks for always supporting my dreams. I love you for that. The fourth acknowledgments is to my daughter Annise Upchurch (Kaiden's Aunt) for always being willing to take care of her niece by making her life as comfortable as possible. I would also like to acknowledge my son David Upchurch (Kaiden's Uncle) for loving Kaiden and always being a support to her. I will give a loving memory to Kaiden's grandmother , the mother of Velvet McClurkin, Francesca Irenes Torres (deceased) I also want to give honorable mention to all of these people because they were instrumental in encouraging my family and I to never give up on Kaiden: Increasing Faith Deliverance Ministries of Sanford, The Peoples Family, My Spiritual Parents (Bishop Charles & Pastor Pattie Mellette), The Greatest Aunt in the World (Judy

Mellette) Pastor Donna Taylor, Mary Jeanette Crump, Eugenia Robinson, Pastor Alice Hooker, Pastor Gail Dickens, The Kinney Family, The Marks Family, The Blue Family, Bishop Jerry & Pastor Teresa Brown, The Lowe Family, Gail Wilson, Kim Warr , Pastor Margaret Rivers and Dara Davis. My gratitude also extends to Pastor Stephanie Genwright, Holly from Bright Horizons, Jennifer Rhyne, Betty Johnson (deceased) and Family, All of Velvet McClurkin's sister's and brother's (Kaiden's uncles and aunts), Dale McLean (Kaiden's Godfather), Floyd L. Knight School Staff, Stepping Stones Learning Center Staff, The ARC Staff in Southern Pines North Carolina, UNC Primary Care Clinic Staff and the PICU Staff at UNC Hospital.

CONTENTS

Foreword 7
Author's Acknowledgements 9

Chapter One   You Never Know What Will Happen In This Life!
[The Day Our Lives Changed Forever] 13

Chapter Two   Moving Forward
[Understanding Kaiden's Health] 21

Chapter Three   Who Is Kaiden?
[She Sees, She Hears, And She Feels] 27

Chapter Four   Looking From The Inside Out
[They Don't See What We See] 31

Chapter Five   Being An Advocate For Kaiden
[Good Looking Out] 37

Chapter Six   Being Patient During The Process
[Learning How To Wait And Not Give-Up!] 43

Chapter Seven   We Thought We Lost Her
[Fighting For Her Life] 47

Chapter Eight   Understanding Kaiden's Purpose
[God's Little Sunshine] 53

Chapter Nine	Making Lasting Memories Of Kaiden [Enjoying Kaiden]	57
Chapter Ten	Things Will Happen But We Must Accept It And Deal With It [Kaiden Is In God's Hand]	63
Chapter Eleven	A Grandmother's Role And The Love I Have For Kaiden [Kaiden Changed My Life]	67
Chapter Twelve	My Affirmation, My Faith In God, And My Miracle [God Did It!]	81

About the Author 95

CHAPTER ONE

YOU NEVER KNOW WHAT WILL HAPPEN IN THIS LIFE!
[The Day Our Lives Changed Forever]

I would've never thought that life would change as fast and as drastically as it did. Sometimes you really don't expect some things to happen in life, and they do. The day our lives changed forever was when my son and his high school girlfriend came and told me that she was pregnant. I would've never thought it would've happened. I knew they were dating, but I never thought it was going any further. As parents, my husband and I have learned that things happen and you have to learn to make adjustments. Well, this was one thing I did not know how I would tell my husband because I knew he had some expectations of my son being a father later on in life. The thing is, what you plan does not always happen. I quickly had to learn to get over the way I wanted things to be.

When my son came and told me that his high school girlfriend was pregnant, he said that his life flashed before him. I asked him what he meant. He said, "Mom, I am afraid. I don't know what

Daddy will say and I know I am too young to be a father. Then he looked at me and said, "Mom, I got her pregnant with our baby and it is my job to take care of my baby." When he said that to me, I knew then my son was a good young daddy. I realized that uncertainty was all around us. I was uncertain about how my husband would feel. I did know that he would encourage my son and his girlfriend to get their education. I just know that for a moment, he would be upset because he always encouraged my son to wait until marriage before becoming a father. Once my son told my husband, my husband let him know his feelings about the situation. My husband is a good understanding father because he let them both know that we were here to help them both. He did have a talk with my son and encouraged him to be a good father, finish high school, and go to college. My son was still in high school and his girlfriend was attending her first year in college. My husband encouraged him to co-parent the baby with his girlfriend. My husband told my son and his girlfriend to stay on pace with their education and not worry about their baby. ALL THEY NEEDED TO KNOW IS THAT THEY HAD OUR HELP!

During the second trimester, my son and I went with his girlfriend to all of her baby appointments. The doctor would always listen to the heartbeat and tell us everything was fine. During this time, my son's girlfriend was in college and we would help her go back and forth to school. We would make sure she and the baby were doing fine. The baby seemed to be fine, and Dad and Mom were preparing themselves for the baby's arrival. As the day got closer, they chose a name for the baby. They said her name would be Kaiden Enjoli Upchurch. We did not realize what was up the road ahead, but that name would really mean something to us. They told me that Kaiden meant warrior and from that day forward, I kept her name close to my heart.

It was now a month before the baby was due and Mommy was feeling ok. She had gotten bigger and knew time was drawing close. The time had come for Kaiden to enter the world. We all waited eagerly. On December 31st, 2009, at 4:29 AM, she came into the world. Her mom and dad experienced the birth of their child; and I realized I was a nana for the first time. One thing that was sticking out in my mind was that during labor she had a hard time pushing Kaiden out. Kaiden's head was too big for her mom to have a regular birth. The doctor prepared for Kaiden's mom to have a caesarean. The caesarean went well. Once Kaiden was born, they tested her just like they did all babies and everything was fine but one thing. The doctor came in the room and let us know that he wanted to send Kaiden to another hospital that could run tests on her. He let us know that he believed that Kaiden had some issues and this hospital was not equipped to test her. The next day, Kaiden was sent to a hospital in Chapel Hill, NC. The hospital did tests on Kaiden and she was diagnosed with something we never believed would ever happen to her.

My family called me when I was at the house heading to see Kaiden. They told me they had something to tell me, but it was best for me to wait until I got to the hospital. I persistently asked my family to tell me what was wrong. They would not tell me. They said that they preferred to talk to me in person about it. So, I drove over to the hospital praying and believing God for his new mercies. When I got to the hospital, they sat me down with all the doctors and the hospital social worker and told me that my granddaughter was diagnosed with hydrocephaly, porencephaly, and cerebral palsy. They first diagnosed her with hydrocephaly which is an abnormal buildup of cerebrospinal fluid in the ventricles of the brain. The danger is that increased pressure could compress and damage her brain. The second diagnosis was porencephaly which is a neurological disorder where she only has a cyst of water in the top hemisphere of her brain. The third diagnosis was cerebral palsy which is a problem with the brain development. She would have reflex movement that cannot be controlled and her muscles would be tight. Lastly, she was diagnosed with having seizures. So, basically, when you get right down to the point, my granddaughter was born with NO BRAIN in the top of her head; only water sits there. The bottom half is in place and it controls her breathing and her heart. It is the grace of God that she would be able to breathe. The prognosis got even worse. They finally told us that she would live to be no more than two-three months old, and that she could die at any time. They let us know she was too young to administer medication so they sent her home. This would be up to God now and we would have to trust God every day for Kaiden. This was a devastating blow for our family. Kaiden's parents were hurt, my daughter was hurt, my baby son was hurt, and so was my husband, and Velvet's family. I was so angry. They sent us home with our baby. There was nothing no one could do about it, but God.

All I could think about was the scripture in Deuteronomy 31:6—be strong and of a good courage, fear not, nor be afraid of them, for the Lord thy God, he it is that do go with thee; he will not fall thee, nor forsake thee(King James' Version). But I was angry because I felt within myself they sent our baby home to die. Only God was the one keeping my mind right now. I told them at the hospital I was afraid to get close to her. I knew my heart would get broken. The more I tried to keep from getting attached to her; the more she attached to me. My granddaughter is so beautiful and the pain of not being able to see her walk and talk like other children was devastating me. Then my heart was hurting for Kaiden's mother and father. They were so disappointed and so was the whole family. Oh my God, what just happened to our family and such a beautiful baby! *God, why have you forsaken us! What do we do now? Where do we go from here? Will she live? Will she die? Does she really have to live like this? God, what is going on? Is this our fault? Did we do something wrong? Is this a curse? I am so upset, God, and I need to know what to do next.* Kaiden's parents were looking to my husband and me for strength. We did not want to let them down. The day of the prognosis, we invited our family, some of Velvet's family, and close friends to rally around us at the hospital for support. We did not tell some family members right away because we were afraid they would not understand. This was my first grandbaby and this is how she was born. What does a person do with this kind of information? I cried. I had feelings of hurt, anger, rejection, fear, and no hope.

But I could never let Kaiden's parents know how afraid I was. I wanted to be strong for them.

I looked at my grandbaby; she looked normal, but she wasn't. At birth, we were told she had no vision. We thought she would be blind. The doctors did not know if she would have vision or not. She did not hear at birth but months later, her hearing was tested and she could hear. It was going to take a miracle for Kaiden to live. Every hospital visit was negative. The doctor did not see any improvements. I even realized that the doctors did not see a future for Kaiden. But I had to stop having a pity party and begin to pray for Kaiden's parents, and all of us, that God will have mercy, and walk in the love that God can give. We tried to purchase an insurance policy and from then until this day no insurance company will insure her.

Our family was broken and a lot of people did not know it. Most people would say we are praying for you and that God is going to heal your granddaughter. Some people would say that this was a test from God and he wanted to see how we handled it. When you are going through a hard time, I have learned that people can say hurtful things and they really don't understand the situation. We made a decision that we would not tell many people about Kaiden's situation. We also made an agreement that as a family, which included Kaiden's mom, we will always put Kaiden's best interests first. We made up in our mind that we would treat her like the princess she was. I had made up in my mind that I would always be there for Kaiden. I promised Kaiden's other grandmother who is now deceased, that I would take care of her. I remember Kaiden's mother saying, "Mrs. Denise, she needs you in her life. Please do not say you won't be close to her." So, from that day on I took my Nana position in Kaiden's life. I made a promise to her mother and father that I would love my grandbaby and do all I could do to help her. I promised them that she can live with my husband while they are in college and even when they get out, we would keep her for as long as they need us to. Our home will always be a place for Kaiden. After Kaiden got home, we all came together in the living room of our house and prayed for Kaiden, ourselves, and that God would see us through this part of her life. We were now considered to be a part of Team Kaiden. Team Kaiden consists of us working together as a team, not worried about our personal issues, putting all differences aside and always keeping her safe and as healthy as we possibly can. We already knew that we would have some bad days and that along the way she may face some difficulties. I always told my children and Kaiden's mama, that Kaiden is God's little sunshine. Kaiden immediately had brought Sunshine in our lives. No matter how bad things were looking and what challenges had begun to come our way, were encouraged to stay the course. I just wanted Kaiden's parents to know that if they keep God first and do what's right, things would turn out good for them. We all had made a point to not look at things as if it was so bad, but look at the fact that God can make a miracle out of this situation. We all began to live our life with Kaiden being a part of it. At this point, Kaiden had turned seven months and she was doing well. She cried at night sometimes because she may not be feeling her best. She had a lot of fluid in her head that needed to be drained. We knew that every month Kaiden was fighting to stay alive. The doctors really didn't understand how Kaiden would develop. They wanted us to understand that it was not promised that she would smile or even recognize who we are. We knew she would never walk or talk, but when they said she may not know who we were, I began to feel depressed. But God began to minister to me and let me know that Kaiden's life was in his hands. I had to repeat that God had Kaiden in his hands, over and over, until I finally realized it was the truth. I even went to therapy because I did not know how things would turn out for Kaiden. The therapy helped me deal with the fact that Kaiden is here. It helped me understand that I have to focus on the good things that were going on with her. When negative things would happen, I would write it down and pray about it instead of worrying about things I could not change. I began to see God moving in her life right then and there. She was making strides and she was not even a year old yet. I would talk to Kaiden for hours and let her know that she was beautiful. I would pray for her, read the Bible to her. I would read books, let her touch things that were soft and hard. I loved to talk to Kaiden. She would always give me eye contact and let Nana know she was listening.

CHAPTER TWO

MOVING FORWARD
[Understanding Kaiden's Health]

Kaiden was now one year old. She was already defying what the doctors believed. I was so happy because now, Kaiden had begun to recognize my voice. At times, she would turn her little head and look around trying to hear who all were in the room. All our children had left and were in college. Kaiden was the only one to stay home with my husband and me. She was a sweet little girl. She did require a lot of assistance. Kaiden had a rocky road between the ages of one and five years.

When she was one year old, we basically had to see what would happen with her. She could not have any surgeries until she was about two years old as it would be a risk. So, they did a lot of x-rays on her and were making sure the fluid in the brain was not overpowering her brain. She cried a lot when she was one year old. I do believe she had a lot of head pain. She really needed a shunt to help the fluid in the brain re-route and she would eventually urinate the fluid out. Basically, we all had to play the waiting game because everything was about her turning two before they did any major surgeries.

When she was two years old, she did get the shunt and it helped her a lot. The hospital that saw to her care was not willing to put the shunt as they felt it was too risky. They referred us to another hospital and they put the shunt in for her. We spoke with the doctor and he let us know he would put the shunt in, and she would be ok. Kaiden did have the surgery and her hair had to get cut short on one side. She awoke from the surgery fine, but the process of healing was very slow. We had to administer strong medication to her for pain; she had to take it every day until she felt better. She cried sometimes and she sleep a lot. After the six weeks recovery was over, they sent her back to her primary hospital and they began to take good care of the shunt. At the age of two and a half, she began to have seizures. Some of the seizures were like ticks, she would shake, turn her body one way, and stare. These were scary, because sometimes, they would make her cry or even laugh. She has had doctors that do not believe in God's miracles, so it was not always easy. They did not make us any promises about her health. There was always the fear that she would not make it, but God continued to show himself strong in her life.

One day, I took Kaiden to an appointment with her newly appointed neurologist. She was negative, and I got fed up. Every appointment, she had something negative to say. I let the doctor know that I understood that she has to tell us the truth about her diagnoses. I had to admit that I did not like her bedside manner and I let her and her supervisor know. I asked the lead attending doctor to assign Kaiden a new neurologist and they did, and to this day that new neurologist has been with Kaiden and has worked along with our family for many years.

Every doctor's appointment she attended, was not easy because there was always a negative report. When we would go to the appointment, at the end they would give us a summary of the things that were wrong with Kaiden. Kaiden is the strongest child I know. According to medical records, she has been diagnosed with infantile cerebral palsy, hydrocephaly (water in the brain), chronic epileptic seizures, anencephaly, acid reflux disease, nasal inflammation due to allergen, seasonal allergic reaction, growth failure, congenital anomaly of the brain, pneumonia, upper respiratory infection, feeding problem, sleep apnea, infection of eye region, porencephaly, difficulty swallowing, anemia, asthma, and low immune system. She has to deal with all of these conditions in her body because of how her diagnoses affects her. She takes over twelve medications that help to sustain her life on a daily basis. The biggest medication she takes, is every day we read the Word of God and pray over her. She is a miracle. Sometimes we have to figure out what is bothering her. She doesn't talk so we have to read her body language and the nurses at the house have to keep up with her stats. We, as a family, had to learn how to take her temperature, read her oxygen levels, and keep up with her pulse rate. We have to figure out if she is in pain or not. This is not always an easy thing to do because it takes studying her body and learning the changes. I have learned my granddaughter and I know when she is sick.

On this page, there is a picture of what Kaiden's brain looks like. This is porencephaly, anencephaly, and hydrocephaly and she has some tissue in the top. Kaiden has no cognitive ability. These brain abnormalities affect her ability to learn, walk, talk or even understand. She does not have a hypothalamus because there is nothing in the top of her brain but a cyst and two empty cavities. The hypothalamus is part of the endocrine systems. It is so unfortunate but she does not have a lot of the needed glands for that system. She is missing the hypothalamus that regulates the body temperature. Kaiden can have a high temperature at the wrong time. She can also have a low temperature and it can cause her to go into shock by being sepsis (having a bad infection). She is also missing the pituitary gland and the pineal gland. These two glands are important because they help with her growth, regulate blood pressure, and also help with controlling dehydration. It also affects her sleeping so she has to take melatonin to help her sleep at night. Kaiden is smaller than normal but there are times she can gain weight fast because she is sedentary. She tends to dehydrate fast so we have to give her plenty of water to drink. We have to keep a close eye on her because of her body's inabilities to function properly. Kaiden has a lot of fluid on the brain, but the shunt helps control the water level in her brain by helping her evacuate it through her urine. She has a very small amount of tissue in the top surrounding her brain and it may possibly help her brain function a little. We really don't know. The bottom cortex is what controls her heart beat, the breathing, and respirations. At birth, if the bottom hemisphere of her brain did not work, then she would have expired when she was born. Kaiden is a real fighter. She has been through so much in her health and she is still fighting today.

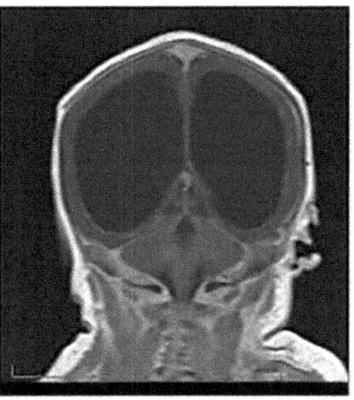

Picture of how Kaiden's brain looks inside

We have been through so many medical scenarios with her. There are times when her body system does not work for her. I know we can't keep her in a plastic bubble and protect her from people and germs, but it is important to protect her as much as possible. I was told by the doctors that for the rest of her life she will have an immune system of a six-month-old. She has no way of protecting herself. When she gets a cold, it shuts her down. It can be a matter of life and death for Kaiden. When she gets a cold, she sleeps a lot. A cold is like getting an infection for her. She also has asthma. When she has an asthma attack, it affects her breathing and she does not sleep well at night. Kaiden has been through periods when she could not urinate for a day or so. Now that was very scary because we did not know what to do. We learned that she has to have a certain amount of fluid intake a day.

During her first five years, she was sick with a lot of upper respiratory infections. She did not have the ability to control her swallowing so this alone was building up fluid in her lungs and we did not know it. She also had difficulty swallowing and we found out that adenoids and tonsils were causing obstructions in her throat. The only thing is she got her tonsils taken out and then it produced a lot of extra saliva. She has to take medication to slow her saliva secretions down. Kaiden has to be suctioned at least five to ten times a day.

During these last five years, she experienced a lot of muscle issues because of cerebral palsy and with muscles tightening all the time. She did receive physical therapy; it helped some but being sedentary predisposed her to tight joints and aches and pains in her body. For years, she has had physical therapy, speech therapy (feeding therapy), and occupational therapy. These different services were beneficial to her and they helped her along the way.

Kaiden has had several surgeries during the first six years of her life. She had dental surgery, tonsillectomy, adenoid surgery, shunt surgery, and a feeding tube. All of the surgeries were successful but there were some issues that arose from the surgeries. I feel like she gets a surgery for one thing but then she ends up getting side effects and other issues come up.

Kaiden went through a stint where she lost a lot of weight. We tried to find what caused it. One of the main issues was that she was not able to consume her food and keep it down. The food she was swallowing led to aspirating and it went down into her lungs. She also could not digest so much food at one time. She went from 29lbs to 24lbs. At that time, she was five years old. This was a scary time for us because if she got any smaller there would be many complications. She was losing weight and unfortunately, it she was not getting any nutrients in her body because she was not getting enough food. The doctors finally let us know she needed surgery because she was getting malnourished. She began to sleep a lot and she did not have any energy. These events led up to surgery and she is doing better now. We have to be watchful and make sure that she doesn't gain too much weight because excessive weight can affect her joints, hips, and bones in her body. If she gains too much weight, we will not be able to lift her.

These years were never easy for her. It has been a pleasure for us to take care of her. God only gives you so many changes to make a mark on the earth; and it is best to do it the right way. We have had fear but we yet trust God. She smiles, and that alone makes me feel confident that she is God's little Sunshine and has pulled through all her surgeries during this time in her life.

CHAPTER THREE

WHO IS KAIDEN?
[SHE SEES, SHE HEARS, AND SHE FEELS]

Who is Kaiden? She is a warrior, a fighter, one who wants to live and really can feel who is around her. *She is a miracle child!* There are three senses that she uses most of the time. She sees well. They did an eye exam on her when she was a toddler. We were told she had peripheral vision only and the vision may not be very clear. There have been times when she would follow us from left to right with her eyes. She has tracked objects from left to right with her eyes. The next of the five senses that are strong is her, is hearing. Kaiden was born unable to hear in both ears. They tested her again a month after she was born and there was some ability of hearing for her. As she grew older, it was easy to call her name and she would look and respond. If she heard a noise, she would turn her head quickly. That was so amazing to us. We were happy to know that not only could she see a little, but also, she could hear. The last sense that was a strong part of her, was touch. Kaiden loved for us to touch her head and rub it. She also liked for us to rub her feet. The touch was good for her. I could tell when we would kiss her on her cheek, she would look up, and looked around and be astounded to feel. I would also buy books that had animals that were made out of soft fury material. Touch is what made her happy. I would take her hand and let her feel the curvature in my face. She loved that, too. Now remember, we were in amazement because she was not supposed to know who we are. She wanted us to communicate with her and she was going to get our attention. It worked. We were excited that she had a way to communicate. I was really feeling that it was better for her to have some system of communication than none. Kaiden did not cry a lot. We had to always try to figure out what was wrong. I truly believe she had a lot of headaches and we did not know it. Once the shunt was placed in her brain, I believe the fluid pressure was not as high and the pain may have diminished.

Kaiden is a very unique child. I know she has diagnoses that really dictate that she should not be alive. But I am so grateful to God! I really believe that Kaiden feels the love and care that is given to her from the people that surround her. Kaiden is surrounded by people every day. She always feels love and care. I know that this is what makes her fight to live. The moment the love leaves and she feels nothing, she may give up because she feels no one speaking into her life. She is always looking for love. She likes to be held and cuddled. The funny thing is that it was speculated by medical professionals that she would not know who we were. We were told that she may not hear, see, feel, laugh, or even know her surroundings. Families that have babies that were diagnosed with the same medical condition have confirmed that their babies do not do what Kaiden does. I have talked to many families and they ask me how my granddaughter is doing and I tell them, good. They are amazed that she knows how to sneeze and cough. There are some children with this diagnosis that do not cough or sneeze.

Kaiden tells a lot of stories with her eyes. It seems to me that her eyes talk to everyone. When she is upset, she makes gestures with her eyes. When she doesn't feel good, you can look at her eyes and they look weak. When she is happy, her eyes light up and become big and bold. When she is wet, she makes her eyes stretch and she will make a coughing sound because she is trying to tell us she is wet. She will cough hard if she wants someone to hold her. She loves to be held. It is so amazing to us that she knows how to communicate.

Kaiden continues to defy doctors. I am so amazed. I realize that it is God that helps her and she learns by the repetitiveness that is used when helping her. We really don't know if she has memory or not. As a family, we try to work with her by keeping her doing the same thing every day. She gets used to it and tends to responds to what we are doing.

Kaiden has feelings. I began to realize that when I read or talk to her and even at times when she would get startled by certain noises. I remember one day, I was yelling at the dog and she jumped; it startled her and she began to cry. I picked her up and comforted her and told her I was sorry for yelling. She is easily startled if we accidently hit the bed. She also reacts to the cartoon, Dora the Explorer. If I put Dora the Explorer video on, Kaiden will listen to it. As soon as she hears Dora's voice, she immediately begins to smile. Dora the Explorer videos will hold her attention for long periods of time. She will listen to it all day if I let her. She never gets tired of hearing Dora's voice. She also likes Mickey Mouse Club House. She smiles a lot. She is generally a happy child. Even when she is sick, she is a good sport. She is the type of child that doesn't show anger. If something bothers her, she will turn her head and ignore us. She also expresses herself when she receives physical therapy. She doesn't like it so she will cry when the physical therapist does exercises on her. She needs physical therapy because her body tends to stiffen over a period of time. She loves to be cuddled. She gets mad if we do not pick her up and cuddle her. She knows how to look sad and that makes us give in to her. It makes us happy to see Kaiden express her feelings because she is really not supposed to be able to do that. It is such a pleasure to watch her do what health professionals said she would not do. This is our Miracle child and we never forget it.

Kaiden is beautiful inside and out. Her personality is so sweet. She will smile at people she knows. Kaiden tends not to smile at strangers. Believe it or not, when she was younger and someone who she did not know changed her pamper, she would cry. We learned then that Kaiden has a personality. Her eyes and her sounds are what make her personality speak for itself. I never treat her different from other children because I want her to blend in. It is hard for her to blend in sometimes because some people don't accept her for who she is.

As a family, we embrace her personality. We embrace the love she gives. We embrace her smile, laughter, and even tears from crying. All of these things she can do, is looked at as milestones. She has come a long way. The little things she does is big things in our eyes. We realize that God has helped her through this process. The process has not been easy but Kaiden is still here with us and she is still fighting to survive. So, we have to fight with her and for her.

One key point about understanding Kaiden is when she hears disagreements, she does not like it. She does not like to hear any type of arguing. If we are watching a game and we disagree about something and we get loud, it makes her upset. She will start coughing or shaking her legs. She has a way of getting her point across. We have to express ourselves in another way. Kaiden definitely has feelings and she has a way of letting us know what she likes or doesn't like. This may seem unbelievable, but it is really real.

CHAPTER FOUR

LOOKING FROM THE INSIDE OUT
[They Don't See What We See]

Kaiden is an exceptional little girl. She has been through a lot of transition in these eight years of her life. She is truly a warrior. When I think about my granddaughter, it brings tears to my eyes. I have tears of pain and of joy. The joy comes from seeing her fight through all of her life difficulties and receiving all the love she can. The pain is when I know she is in physical pain and there is nothing I can do about it.

Some people don't see Kaiden the way we see her. There are times I have been frustrated because she was not treated with respect. I ask God why some people mistreat children that have special needs or are disabled. I have even had to pray that I would not lose my temper with them. I do understand that they may not understand Kaiden's diagnoses or they just don't know what she is living with. I watch children and adults stare at her. Some have even stood in her face, stared at her, and said absolutely nothing. I always wish they would at least say hello or something. I can understand young children that don't understand. I know there are adults that don't understand and maybe I shouldn't get offended. When they stare, I begin to speak and ask questions. I often tell children that Kaiden is just like them and she just doesn't walk and talk. I take time and show them how she will smile and even enjoy hearing their voice.

I will never forget the day my daughter and I went into a department store to buy Kaiden some clothes. We were enjoying ourselves until an older woman reached over Kaiden and almost pushed her buggy into her wheel chair stroller. The woman did not apologize and she acted as if Kaiden was not even there. My daughter turned around and said, "Excuse me, madam." The lady rolled her eyes at my daughter and pushed her buggy off as if she had not done anything wrong. I encouraged my daughter not to worry about it and let it go. It was very frustrating to see how Kaiden was being mistreated. Kaiden faces rejection at times. There are people that have no regards not only for Kaiden, but they don't regard her family either.

There have been people in the medical field that sometimes forget that Kaiden and our family have feelings, too. There was a time when one of the doctors said that they never realized how big Kaiden's head was. She kept making that point but never explained why she was saying it. I interjected and let the doctor know that as many times as she had seen Kaiden, she never noticed her head. I told her that I did realize her head was big and it is like that because of the diagnoses she was given at birth. This doctor did not understand this because they were not a neurologist, they were another type of doctor. I encouraged them to read up on Kaiden's diagnoses.

There are times that we may go to a restaurant and Kaiden would accompany us there. I watch so many people that would stare at her and never speak. Some of them would stare at her if she coughs or make any noises. I would always say hello to the person that was staring her, and I would ask them how they were doing. Kaiden has sat with a group of children, listening to a story and the orator did not even acknowledge Kaiden, but she acknowledged the other children.

One of the major things that made me upset was when a group of children were picking at Kaiden and the fact that she was in a wheel chair. We were at the school in the park area and after school, I went to their parents and I told them what happened. One mother apologized for her son making fun at Kaiden, but the other mom did not believe her son did that. I told the mom right in front of her son that it was not right and I would let the school know if he did it again. This was so awful and I realize then that I had to forgive and not have a grudge in my heart. I do understand that people come from different family backgrounds and everyone is not the same, but we made up in our minds that we will stand with her and talk to those that treat her different. Yes, she is different because of how she was born at birth, but she still has feelings like everyone else. We want her treated with dignity and respect.

As a team of caregivers, it is our job to protect Kaiden in every way. She may not have the cognitive ability like other children, but she still feels, and when people direct their words toward her, she pays attention. Kaiden has been the recipient of some negative energy toward her. I try to address it in a kind way and I ask parents to allow me to explain to their children what my granddaughter was born with. We are not ashamed of Kaiden. I feel that people have to learn about the world she lives in. She doesn't have to come up to their level, they have to come up to hers. My goal is to educate and encourage people to read about her and learn that she is not like any other child. She has her own identity.

I always encourage my family to try to be the bigger person and look over some things, especially when it comes from smaller children. Adults are a different story and they are the ones we have to address as nice as we possibly can.

It is so important that children with special needs are understood just like other children. Kaiden is no different from other children. She was born with disabilities that affect her quality of life. She is one of the bravest little girls I have ever known. She may not know people individually but she knows when she has entered another environment that is not hers. She gets very quiet and withdrawn when she comes around people she doesn't know. Believe it or not, she can tell when someone is around her and they do not have a good attitude or may have bad behavior. She will breathe hard to let us know she is very uncomfortable. You know, I realize that some people have not experienced what we have so, they may not understand the importance of protecting a child with special needs. Some people are on the outside looking in and just because Kaiden doesn't speak, she still can feel the hearts of people. She notices when people stand in her face and stare and don't speak to her. I always ask people to please say hello to my granddaughter. People looking from the outside in should take one day and put themselves in the shoes of our family and they will see the struggles, the hope, the love, the joys, the frustrations, the fears, the faith, and even the reason why Kaiden was born to be an example for other children with these types of struggles. Yes, from the outside, everything about Kaiden may look easy, but she has a lot of complicated issues that keep us on our toes. So, the next time someone looks at her and doesn't really see who she is, they need to take another look and see who she really is.

We do understand that people may not see Kaiden like we do. Some people may have sympathy, but they don't understand what she is going through. There are people that may not be looking from the inside out at her situation, but they realize that she is facing many things. There are people that always encourage our family and they always say they are praying for Kaiden. I do let them know we appreciate their prayers. God has truly helped us to make the adjustments we need to make to take care of Kaiden. There are times I want to go into detail about Kaiden's situation if they do not understand. There are some people I choose to tell because they need to know that there are times when she is invited to events that she is unable to attend. The fact that she doesn't to attend many events, they ask her what is wrong and is everything ok with her. This alone makes me have to explain myself to them.

When we finally share Kaiden's situation with others, it seems hard to believe it. I really understand that, too. The images of a child having absence of a part of their brain is truly hard to fathom. But it is real, and some people really get scared when I tell them. They begin to ask me so many questions. Some people want to know how she lives like that. What is Kaiden's life expectancy? Will her brain grow back? I appreciate that they feel comfortable to ask those questions. I want them to know what it feels like and have an understanding that yes, in some ways she is different from other children. All Kaiden wants, is to be loved and feel loved. She is always ready to receive hugs, smiles, and kind words from people. I have to look at it from both views, from the inside out and the outside in, because each view has to be understood and when there is understanding, people can relate to and understand her.

Families of children with special needs are sometimes misunderstood. People tend to look at what they see but they don't take the time to encourage these families. I want to express and appreciate all the prayers and encouragements we can get from them to help. They help us face tomorrow. We are not afraid of what the future holds for Kaiden. We try to take it one day at a time. Some people don't even know what we face day to day. But if they could see what we see, they would understand that there is a lot going on and we need prayers, love, and support.

I hope you can see what I see about Kaiden. I tried to give you a view. This alone may help everyone understand. I really believe that when we ask questions, we will get answers. I like to be asked questions about Kaiden. This will help people understand who she really is and how she can be seen if we take the time to understand her make up.

CHAPTER FIVE

BEING AN ADVOCATE FOR KAIDEN
[Good Looking Out]

Kaiden has so many people that advocate for her. Being her grandmother, I choose to be one of her biggest advocates. Kaiden has a team that works for her best interest. We are a team but yet, family. Kaiden sees people as family when she gets to know them. She doesn't know anything else. She has lived with me for years and this is her special environment where she is not afraid to express herself. I have been taking care of her since she was a baby. As her advocate, I choose to intervene for her in every situation if possible. I have also been an advocate on behalf of her mother and father. I love advocating for Kaiden because I want to make sure that all her needs are met.

When a child has disabilities, it is important that the advocate understands what is going on in the life of the child. Kaiden has many medical needs. It is important, as an advocate, that there is continual communication with the doctors and all health care professionals that are responsible for her health. I have had to talk to Kaiden's primary care doctors, her doctors that are specialists, physical therapist, speech therapist, orthopedics, dentists, surgeons, nutritionists, pharmacists, hospital social workers, case managers, home health equipment salesmen, home health agency providers, and all those who are responsible for her educational needs. I have sat in meetings and discussed what is best for her on behalf of her parents. There has to be an understanding between parents and grandparents to know that when the parents are not available because of college, work or other issues, that other family can stand in and help. I and my daughter have been two of Kaiden's biggest advocates. Kaiden's parents do come to some meetings when feasible. They have trusted me for years to advocate on her behalf and it has been a pleasure.

An advocate has to be willing to stand in the gap and speak on behalf of the child. Kaiden doesn't have the ability to speak up for herself but we will. I have met with so many health professionals and they feel that because they are an expertise in that field, they may know what is best for Kaiden. Eventually, they come back and ask us how we feel the situation should be handled. If the doctors make a medical decision then we only intervene if we feel we need a second opinion. There have been times when I had to tell some health care professionals that she was tired or some things will not work for her. I have also had to let some professionals know that Kaiden does not like certain things and how her body reacts to certain situations. Most doctors always tell us that they need our input because we know her better than they do. That makes me feel good. We are not medical doctors but we have learned everything that is needed to take care of Kaiden.

There have been times when we have switched doctors because their bedside manner was not the best. We have also switched when a health care professional ignored Kaiden or made it seem that our feelings about her were not important enough. When there is a decision that has to be made about her care, if we deem it necessary, we will ask more than one doctor. Kaiden has a team of doctors and we have to make sure that we make them aware of our activities in all medical decisions that will be made. Every time she has had surgery, we ask a lot of questions before and after every surgical procedure. We have learned that there are no ignorant questions. We have to be aware of everything that may happen to her. We also had to advocate by explaining to the nurses that just because one child has the same diagnoses as another, it doesn't mean they will respond the same. The advocate knows the child well and they can tell when they behave different than usual. One thing I have learned is that the greatest trainer for any professional is the family. The family knows the child and how they work. They understand the child's disposition and the dynamics of how she is affected in any social environment. They know when she's up and they know when she feels down.

I have also had to advocate for her when it comes to her education. I wanted to make sure that she would be home-schooled. Kaiden has a weak immune system. Every time she goes to school, she gets sick. School is a great place, but Kaiden just cannot handle the high rate of germs. She cannot guard her body against it. I have been told that Kaiden has the immune system of a sixth-month-old baby. I really believe that. She cannot come around sick people. As soon as she has been around them, she usually catches whatever sickness they have such as a cold, pneumonia, fever, flu, and any other types of upper respiratory issues. We learned that going to public school has been a lot for her at this point in her life. I have been to IEP meetings and let them know that she cannot be in school more than a certain number of hours. There are times that Kaiden has awaken and was weak, no energy and really sleepy. I knew then she would not be able to go school and I had to call and get a note for a few days so she could stay out of school and re-cooperate. We always want her to get better and these are the decisions that have to be made to get her healthy or back to normal.

As advocates, we do what we can do to make sure Kaiden's life is comfortable, she can rest easy, and that she is safe.

I believe that we get only so many chances to make a different in someone's life. This is my opportunity to advocate for my granddaughter and I want to do my very best. Every decision we make is important because her life depends on it. We don't get to make mistakes with Kaiden. Kaiden has to have people caring for her who are up on what she needs. We have to make sure that all her needs are met. We have to make sure she gets everything she needs. We have to be animate about getting her to all her appointments on time, take medications on time, and getting the rest she needs for being well. If we continue to do our part, we are helping her get stronger.

Advocating for Kaiden has trained me to have a strong voice for her. I am not afraid to let people know what she needs to keep her well. Advocating for Kaiden means, at all times, we have to be up on all of her medical history. We have to be up on all her physical history. We have to be up on all her family history. We have to know her well. She has been diagnosed with over twelve medical conditions and we have to understand all twelve of them in order to know how to properly tell when something is wrong with her. I feel like I am a Kaidenologist. Kaidenology is the study of Kaiden and how her body works. She is teaching us so much. The more we learn about her, it teaches us how to better advocate for and serve her. She is amazing, and her resiliency is more incredible than anything I have ever seen. I know when she is feeling strong and when she is weak. I have to know it in order to know how to best take care of her on that day.

Being Kaiden's advocate has afforded us the opportunity to share information about her medical conditions with other people. Kaiden has survived for the last year because of the strongest caregiver team a child could ever have. It takes a team to care for her. God has always been first, then he has given her a good family and others that give Kaiden the best care. It is never easy making decisions but we always seek God through prayer and he has always led us in the right direction. Proverbs 3:6—7 has admonished us to trust in God and lean not to our own understanding. We have to acknowledge him in all our ways and he will direct our paths. He always directs us with Kaiden. It is a blessing to be an advocate for her and we have to remain focused and trust God to help us continue to lead her in the right direction.

God will always lead and guide us into a straight path and help us to figure out which way to go. When it comes to Kaiden, we cannot make decisions on our own; it takes the help of God by praying and seeking his guidance. Advocating for her, is team effort. If the family does not understand the needs of the child, it will cause conflict and confrontations. Advocating takes having the pieces to the puzzle and truly understanding how to put the pieces together. Sometimes there are decisions that arise and the family has to say yes or no. When it is yes, it sometimes is easy to say, but when it is no, it's hard because it may seem like it is something that needs to be a yes.

Our family has been in positions that made us question the health care providers. We have weighed out what the doctor said by getting a second opinion and making sure it is not another way to do something. Also, as advocates, we have spoken to a team of doctors for Kaiden, making sure that there is more than one doctor making a major decision. Most of our experiences have been good. We have had a few where we had to let a doctor know we did not agree with them.

One thing the doctors have always told us is that they look to us to tell them how Kaiden is and how she reacts to things. They always say we are the best teacher. There are times that we have worked with other healthcare professionals such as nurses; I would try to tell them about Kaiden and they wouldn't listen. Eventually, they would have to come back and tell us that they needed our help with understanding how Kaiden responds to certain things.

I was also Kaiden's advocate at her school and dealing with the educational professionals. There were times when I would let her teachers know that Kaiden was the type of child that you cannot do certain floor activities with and they did not respectfully listen. It was very unfortunate because she ended up having so many seizures and those activities had to cease until she could get stable. It is important that family advocates for their loved ones, no matter what.

CHAPTER SIX

BEING PATIENT DURING THE PROCESS
[LEARNING HOW TO WAIT AND NOT GIVE-UP!]

WAITING FOR THINGS TO change is not always easy. Kaiden has been through so much and waiting for things to change seems as if it takes forever. Every time I feel like everything is ok, then I may get a bad feeling about Kaiden. I tend to look and say, God, why does my granddaughter have to be like this. I thought I had come to grips with it. But every now and then I have a bad moment.

One day, I had a bad moment. I went to the park to walk and I did not have my granddaughter with me. I sat down and looked over at the swings and see-saw and I saw the children playing. I immediately thought about my granddaughter. All I felt was, Lord, I would love to see Kaiden get down and run around and play with the other children. All I could think about is that she can't run, she can't walk, and she can't talk. I was like, why and how did this happen. All I kept feeling was that my granddaughter is a pretty little girl and she has to spend her life living in a wheel chair and laying around and never get up. I think about her situation a lot. I had to go pray because I began to feel a little depressed. Once I got up and began to focus on other things, I began to focus on the fact that she is still here with us.

I love everything about her and I let her know it. The waiting period when she is overcoming sickness can be long. The Bible says in Psalms 27:14 vs, "to wait on the Lord be of good courage and he shall strengthen thine heart: wait, I say, on the Lord." You got to wait, I got wait. There is anointing in the waiting period. It doesn't feel like, but it's true. When it comes to Kaiden, we have to have patience.

What does it feel when I am about to give up? I don't know what to do about Kaiden's situation. I feel like there is nothing else I can do to make things better for her parents. I do understand that Kaiden is in God's hand, but the reality is that we have to stand on what God says about her. I know God has a good expected end for her but I got to remember not to be afraid when different things happen to her. I am so proud of the family.

Learning how to be patient when you are waiting for God to make some moves in in your granddaughter's life, is not simple. It is a thing that I have to pray about. I used to worry about Kaiden, but I am learning she is in the hand of God and he has her life in control.

A caregiver must learn to wait. Waiting is hard because I am the type of person that likes to fix things myself. I know God has not forgotten about my granddaughter. I just wanted her to be a normal child. She is normal to a certain extent but I just want her to be able to do what other children do. I have had to deal with my understanding and remind myself of the medical issues she has.

Her situation does look bleak but God has been there since she was born. I had to learn to trust in God and wait on him. We all have to be patient with Kaiden. She may not feel the same way every day. Sometimes she feels well, and sometimes she doesn't. Kaiden is the type of child who cannot tell you how she feels. We learn to get to know Kaiden and the way she works.

Some days, Kaiden wakes up and she is not in a good mood. There are times when we do not know what is wrong with her; we have to figure it out. She is not able to tell us. We can take a look at all the symptoms from her diagnoses and try to figure out what is wrong. There are times when the doctor doesn't really know what's wrong. This is very frustrating because we know there is nothing we can change about Kaiden's brain; we have to pray, and this makes a difference. So, the little things about her we make a big deal, because at times it has been a matter of life and death. We don't want death. Sometimes, it's hard to tell what is wrong with Kaiden because she is not a crier at all. She will look at you with her big, bold beautiful eyes with a crazy stare. We have to read her body language, voice sounds, and even be able to tell if she is sleepy. Kaiden is the type of child that doesn't give up. If she is wet she is going to cough to let you know that is feeling very uncomfortable. She also stretches her body and lets us know by movement that she is tired. She has a major way to communicate with us.

There is hope for Kaiden. We all cannot give up. As long as we believe for her, she may continue to believe for herself. She is so great and her personality is so cool. All I can say is that we are willing to fight and help her reach the greatest levels that God has set for her in this life. We all don't know the amount of time we have on earth with Kaiden. We all want to make the best of it, and we realize that love is what will get Kaiden through. Our faith in the Lord, God, will definitely give us hope. Waiting on God patiently, is key. I have to have faith. Fear may try to set in but I realize the Bible says in Hebrews 11:1, "Now faith is the substance of things hope for the evidence of things not seen. We are so expected to have faith and keep the faith."

We always speak good words over Kaiden. We always speak life. Proverbs 18:21 says, "The tongue has the power to speak life and death, and those who love it will eat its fruit." This is why we have to speak good words over her life. We make sure that our friends and family know to speak good things over her. She is Kaiden and we can have faith and hope for her. She deserves to have people that will fight for her well-being. As long as we can get a smile out of her, it fills our hearts with joy.

Sometimes, along the way, there are little bitty hospital scares that come up with Kaiden. One thing that really had us overly concerned was that Kaiden's body would overheat and cool down too low at times. It is scary because at first, we did not know what was causing it. Once we found out that it was her brain, we understood. The brain abnormality (anencephaly, porencephaly and hydrocephaly) has caused some changes in her body. Her hormones do not function like a regular little girl's, should. She also has times when her pulse will run too high and sometimes too low. She also has a hard time getting to sleep, but then there are times she sleeps a long time. I have seen times when Kaiden would also get sad for about an hour, then about an hour later, she would be happy.

Kaiden has feelings and I am always cognitive of that. She is the type of child for whom people do mean something. If I sit around Kaiden quiet and don't talk, she will cough and you can look at her and tell she is worried whether we are around or not. She loves her family and her eyes speak the love she has for us. I have seen her struggle with seizures and ticks and how they affect her body. The cerebral palsy affects her body's muscles. She has days when she is sore and does not like to be picked up or touched. I can tell when she makes noises or her pulse rate goes up because of pain. The epilepsy can make her sleepy. She gets really sleepy because of the seizures. Kaiden has had multiple seizures, but they have only lasted seconds at a time. Kaiden has been through so much. It is important that we be patient. She deserves to have a family that loves her and understands this is a process.

She is God's little Sunshine, and it is important that we continue to understand that she needs her loved ones to be patient. All families have to deal with their child the best way they know how.

CHAPTER SEVEN

WE THOUGHT WE LOST HER
[Fighting For Her Life]

In September 2017, it was one of the most difficult times in our lives. Kaiden got sick and she was having a hard time breathing; we thought it was a cold. We took her to a primary care doctor and all her symptoms were a virus-like cold. The doctor said her lungs did not sound bad. So, she continued to be sick during that week, and one night we observed her breathing too hard and having a hard time sleeping. My daughter and I knew something wasn't right. Kaiden has a lot of complex issues so it is hard to tell when she is dealing with something other than a cold. We took her to the emergency room and found out that she had pneumonia. They immediately admitted her to the hospital and sent her to the PICU, which is pediatric intensive care unit. We really did not know how serious this was. But later that night, we found out that she had pneumonia in her lungs and one side was worse than the other. They let us know that she was not doing well and that this infection was a new strand that had not been seen. We were so afraid because the prognosis was not good. All the doctors were letting us know that she would have to be put on a breathing machine because she was not breathing well. We were told that she could pull through but it would take some time. I knew then, my granddaughter was in distress and if God did not help her, these babies with complex issues usually do not pull through. There were times I thought she would not make it through the night without being on the breathing machine. But I thank God she had one of the best hospitals in the United States taking care of her.

There were days that we were down because we couldn't get her body to respond to the medication and other techniques they were trying to help get her stable. It was very sad and we really were trusting now more than ever. I watched her breathing go from strong to shallow. She tended to sleep a lot because they had her in a deep sleep so her body could rest and so she would not get agitated by the breathing tube. She did not like the breathing tube. It was a tube that was placed down her throat and it would help her breath. I know that it was painful at times. The hardest part for me was that when I would come and see her and start talking to her, she would cry. I hated to talk to her because she wanted me to pick her up and I couldn't. Kaiden's first month in the hospital was the hardest. She was such a good trooper. Every now and then we could get a big smile out of her. The doctors would give us a play by play about her health. When they would make their rounds, we would join in the meeting with all the other doctors. There was a team of doctors that was responsible for her care. After the first month, the doctors tried to take her off the breathing machine, but she was still struggling with her breathing. She was taken off the breathing machine and put back on it about three times. At the end, we were so discouraged because we did not know what was going to happen to her. It seemed as if we were at a dead end and I felt myself giving up. I said, God, I have believed you all these years for my granddaughter please help me not to give up now. I was fainting in my heart. Truth be told, I was afraid. I will admit it. I was afraid, but it doesn't mean I was not trusting God. I had to recall the times that I was afraid during Kaiden's toddler years, but

I still was trusting God. I had to remember how I would encourage Kaiden's father and mother to trust God even when I was afraid, but yet I believed God. I asked God why this terrible thing was happening to my granddaughter. Why is she struggling with this now? I began to get upset. I recalled to God how she was born and had so many complex issues. This is my only living grandchild and I hate to see her suffer and fight like this. These were feelings I had inside. I didn't say anything to my family, but I would go off by myself and cry. I couldn't take seeing all the tubes going into her body. I was so overwhelmed that I really began to feel depressed. Nothing was working.

My heart went out to both her mother and father. I sometimes could not bear seeing them upset or crying. Kaiden's aunt stayed in the hospital with her the whole time. I could not bear seeing her upset. There were times when my husband and I would get upset and cry but we still were keeping the faith that God will bring her through. I realize that God did not love me any less because every now and then my faith would get a little weak. But God would speak to me and say, if I have seen Kaiden through other things, I will see her through this. I do realize that sometimes afflictions will come, but God will deliver us out of them all.

One thing I realize is that everybody's struggles are not the same. Sometimes, people cannot understand what someone else goes through and why. I had a lady ask me a question about if I was a Christian why would God let my granddaughter go through this? I told her that we are still human and still have a body of flesh. We may be born with complex health issues, we may get sick with complex health issues because we still have a human body. This human body is not perfect and we can fall privy to illnesses and diseases. We have a right to believe God to heal us and he can; and if we don't get healed, it doesn't mean something is wrong with us. I do believe that Kaiden is still here because of the miracle working power of God. Our faith in God has brought Kaiden a long way. Prayer and trusting God and believing in God's Word has helped us keep faith, hope, and trust in God. I was still seeing the hand of God move in Kaiden's life during this difficult time. Every now and then the doctor would come into our room and talk like Kaiden was having a setback instead of doing better. During these times, I was very vulnerable and I began to feel I wasn't praying hard enough for my granddaughter. All I could see was Kaiden and how her body wouldn't respond to what was being administered to her. There was one point when Kaiden's kidneys began to fail her. Then her liver was giving her problems too. All I could find myself doing was praying hard and crying out to God about her body. Then her body began to slowly do what it is supposed to do. After a while, her lungs would clear, but then they would refill with secretions again. So, her mother and father asked the doctors would she ever get better. They finally had a meeting with us and told us that she needed a tracheostomy. I really did not understand exactly what that was but I knew it was a surgery that would affect her breathing. They basically said she needed a trachea and that it was going to help her breath once again. The hospital let us know that this was a very big decision for a family to make. Her mother and father did not hesitate to get the surgery for her. I understand that the social workers and doctors have to let us know that getting a trachea will be a lot of work for our family. Our family has always worked together to make her life as comfortable as possible. When I say family, I am talking about the team of people that work around the clock to make Kaiden's life enjoyable. Basically, Kaiden has a team of caregivers that consists of good people that love her and will do whatever they need to help her. We all never complain. We actually realize that sometimes it may get hard, but when you love someone you do whatever you have to do for them to live. If she did not get the trachea, we were not willing to let her suffer or stay on a breathing machine until she could breathe on her own. So, the decision was made; she got her trachea and we were on our way to care for her. We knew when she got the trachea that we would have nurses to come in and take care of her. A trachea has to be properly cared for and you have to have patience. Over the years, we all have learned how to take care of Kaiden. We are always eager to learn and understand what it takes to make her body function properly. Kaiden was fortunate to get a trachea that did not have to be connected to a ventilator (breathing machine). So, we have been trained on how to care for her trachea and she is coming along very well. She has days when she still does not feel her best. But she made it through a very tough time in her life. It was touch and go when she got sick. She stayed in the hospital two months, fighting for her life. She is one of the strongest little girls I know. She is always ready to greet all her visitors with a smile and she will do a small chuckle when something is really funny to her. She knows her surroundings well.

I told God, thank you, for allowing Kaiden to live through this time in her life. It did not look like she would make it, but she did. She has made an adjustment and I always let her know that we care about her. When she first got the trachea, I could tell she was very afraid. She would hear the sounds of us suctioning her trachea. She also can feel it when we change her trachea. I can tell she looked a little confused because it felt so different. She has slowly but surely made her adjustments to having a trachea. Some days she may not feel her best, but she continues to fight. We do all we can do to keep her away from people that may have colds or the flu. Kaiden has allergies so I have to keep the house germ free for her.

Kaiden is so amazing. She went through this storm in her life with grace. I have been around adults that complain and get mad about life. I realize Kaiden may not understand everything that goes on but she understands more than what we give her credit for. She is a phenomenal little eight-year-old girl that can teach other people how to be graceful during their storm. She is definitely God's little Sunshine. Keep shining, Kaiden, you are doing a good job.

Talking about Kaiden's life gives me a lot of pleasure because I am grateful that God has kept her alive and that she is so amazing. There may be other struggles that she faces but one things for sure, as a family, we have learned to handle it gracefully.

Kaiden had so much support during her time in the hospital and it was important that she could hear the voices and feel the touch of those that love her. People came far and near to visit her while she was in the hospital. They donated to the family. People brought us food, offered gift cards that helped us financially.

As her grandmother, I traveled every day to see her if I could. I never wanted her to miss hearing my voices. I would make sure during my time away that I would call and let her hear my voice. She deserves love and support because she is so precious to God, family, and people everywhere.

CHAPTER EIGHT

UNDERSTANDING KAIDEN'S PURPOSE
[God's Little Sunshine]

I WILL ADMIT, AT first, when I found out how Kaiden was born, I was angry. I felt like this was unfair to our family. Well, I had to pray and seek God. Kaiden has lived with me the last eight years of her life and I have seen her go from level to level. She has overcame so much. Kaiden never gives up and she is still here. So, about three years ago, I realized that Kaiden had a purpose for being here. I realized that Kaiden is a very special child. It doesn't matter whether somebody tells her or not, she is so special to us all. She has touched all of our lives in many ways.

I believe she is special because it was told to us that one in ten thousand children are born with what Kaiden has been diagnosed with. It has not been easy to watch her struggle with these health issues. We were also told most children do not live to be her age and some of them die early from respiratory issues. Yes, Kaiden has had some rough times. I feel she is like a ray of sunshine. When my day is bad, I think about all she has been through and how she is still here and it makes me realize I need to be grateful.

I feel that my granddaughter is an example for many families with children just like her. I feel that when they see Kaiden and hear her story, that encourages them that there is hope. There is hope but Kaiden's story helps other families understand what it takes to overcome some obstacles. I do realize that no child is the same. I do know that no one has the same story, but some things that Kaiden has been through may help the family understand the process of what they are going through. We have a lot to share about Kaiden's life. Her story began when she was a new born. We worked along with doctors for all her diagnoses, community outreach workers, social workers, Medicaid workers, social security workers, child development association, dentist, physical therapist, pharmacist, teachers, nurses, nutritionist, speech therapist, home health agencies, school for the blind, and case management workers. We have worked along with all these providers over the years to make Kaiden's life as comfortable as possible. We made sure we kept all her appointments. I always made sure she got things she needed such as pampers, generators, milk, medications, bed pads, beds, wheel chairs, car seats, and body braces (for legs, feet, hands, and arms). Over the years, I have made contact with people who can get my granddaughter the things she needs. It is so important when you have a child with special needs, that you get them all the resources possible. I was able to research about different things that were offered for free to my granddaughter because of her special needs. Then, I networked with other people that have children that were older and they help me avoid some of the pitfalls that they did. I want to help families avoid pitfalls and share information on how I got help for my granddaughter before she left the hospital and after she was born. I always let Kaiden's mother and father know about resources so that Kaiden will always have the things she needs. It is important that she be able to live as comfortably as possible.

One thing about the community when Kaiden was in the hospital—the majority of the community that knew her was praying and even if they didn't know her, they saw her and prayed for her. She has been the poster girl for so many organizations. She has let people know that she may have been born with special needs, but she is here to help the world know that God is able.

Kaiden is here to show forth God's miracle working power. She is showing the world that God works miracles. She is an example to those who do not believe that God can work in her life. She could've been dead a long time ago. God said no, so, she is still here, and I want families to know that there are people that care. The network of caring is so important. I do know you have to stay focused, and keep your mind on God. I do believe in the goal and Kaiden's assignment. This to help children in other families understand the process that she went through. I also want families to know that sometimes it is a challenge, but when you have made up in your mind that that you will do all you need to do for your loved one, then the loved one will fight for life. Kaiden fights for life every day. She loves her parents, her grandparents, aunties, uncles, cousins, other family, and friends.

CHAPTER NINE

MAKING LASTING MEMORIES OF KAIDEN
[Enjoying Kaiden]

I AM ALWAYS MAKING memories of Kaiden. Kaiden's parents constantly make memories of her, and her auntie too. Memories are important because we always want to remember our loved one. Kaiden's life expectancy is not like that of a normal child. We always trust God for extended life. But we realize that in the event of changes taking place in her life, we need something that people can remember her by. I encourage families if they can take pictures. We have created so many keep sakes for her. These keepsakes keep us close to her.

It is so important that families make memories. Kaiden has had an amazing life considering what she has been through. We are always thinking about things we can do to help Kaiden enjoy her life. We spend time taking Kaiden for walks in the park. We also take her to events that will help her to develop her social skills with people. We have also taken her on a cruise, she has traveled overseas, by boat. She has experienced some things in life even if she doesn't understand are happening.

We took her to Mexico by boat before her health changed and she received a trachea. It is not safe to travel with her too far now. She is truly our sweetie and she is important to keep safe. During our boat travels to Mexico, she was very alert, awake and looking at everything she could get her eyes on. She was a little bit more verbal than she is now. She had a way of making loud sounds and telling us no in her own words. We took very good care of her. She had her new stroller and we kept her with us everywhere we went. We took her on the deck of the cruise ship to listen to music and she like it. She really enjoyed the sound of the ocean waves and the feel of the wind blowing on her skin. This was the most I saw her smile and even chuckle. We took her out and strolled her around the city called Cozumel in Mexico. I watched so many people that looked at her. One of the natives of the country told me that any children born in their country with disabilities did not get the help my granddaughter receives. I am so thankful to be in a country that has helped our family and me with the care of my granddaughter.

Kaiden has also traveled to several beaches over the years before she got her trachea. She was a good sport. She always seemed to enjoy the sound of the seagulls, birds chirping and other loud sounds. I could tell she enjoyed the sun on her face and other parts of her skin. She would look around. I know she has vision, but she only has peripheral vision. I would often pick up the warm sand and let her touch it. She also never liked the feel of the water at the beach. The water felt cold on her skin. She would often make a face or whine a little because she did not like it. I would also let her touch the seashells and let her feel the rough texture. There were little pebbles in the sand that I would let her touch too. I could tell she liked the idea of feeling things. She has a high sensory response when it comes to touch and hearing. She can hear the smallest sounds and she will turn her head as quick as she can to see what is in her view. She would also sit and listen to the children and adults play in the ocean water. This would make her smile. She loves being around people. She likes hearing people talk and she loves to be loved by people. There were times when she would look at us and stare us down, because she was trying to figure out what we were doing.

There was another time we were on the beach and she would hear the people singing and just be ecstatic. She loves sounds, voices, singing, talking, and even musical instruments. She loves music and that is a part of who she is. The lights on the beach were the highlight for her.

I often buy her books that has inserts of soft pieces of fabric in them. When I take her hand and rub across the fabric while talking to her, she gives a big smile. She loves books and reading to her is a memory that should never be forgotten.

I also remember the time before she got her trachea; she was so happy about going to the fair. Kaiden loves it because she gets to touch some of the baby chicks. I can remember her smiling and making funny sounds. I also remember the time her aunt, Annise, put her on the pony while walking slowly in a circle. I can remember her looking around and then looking down at the pony. I was on the other side of the pony holding her head back up so she can stay positioned in place. It was phenomenal. She had a smile that set my heart on fire. It's like she knew that she was having fun. Then after the riding the pony, we put her on a little kiddie ride that required us to hold her in our lap but there was no danger because we were in a separate car. It was fun. I could remember her smiling and looking up into the sky. They were playing music and I could remember her looking and listening to the music. Kaiden can be so funny at times. Her facial expression can pierce the heart and make you feel as if you were a million dollar.

I remember the time her mom and aunt took her to get her ears pierced. I choose not to go. I did not want to see her cry. My daughter recorded on her cell phone and sent it to me, anyway (LOL). So, once I got the recording and opened it, I realized Kaiden did fine until they pierced the ear; she squalled and cried and watching it, I found myself crying too. Her mom looked like she was crying, and my daughter too. But now the ears are pierced and Kaiden looks so beautiful with the piercings in her ear.

There have been several occasions that we let her listen to a CD set on her ears. As you watch Kaiden, you will notice that she is the type that will listen and smile or laugh. She really likes Mickey Mouse club house music a lot. Every time she listens to it, she will actually laugh or even smile very hard. She also likes to watch Dora on her tablet. When she hears Dora's voice, she lights up. Dora is a cartoon character that most children really love. Dora can speak English and Spanish. Kaiden knows Dora's voice well. She will listen to Dora for hours and respond with her eyes and sometimes she will extend her legs and move her arms. It is such excitement to see Kaiden respond to Dora and see that she really likes her a lot.

There was a time that Kaiden went to the strawberry patch. She heard the voices of the children and you can tell she really enjoyed herself a lot. We pushed her through the strawberry patch and I let her feel the roughness of the strawberries. I also put the strawberry up to her nose to let her smell it She knew something was going on but she didn't know what is was. She also got to touch the pumpkins, pumpkin seeks, sweet potatoes, and we even let her taste the sweet potatoes on her tongue. I think she liked it. Kaiden is such a blast. For us to have been told she would never smile, feel, or hear; this is truly a miracle.

Kaiden has so many beautiful pictures that we have taken of her. We have made a choice to take as many pictures of her that we can. She has been to photo shoots, personal photographers, and even got her pictures taken at school. We have created several picture collages of her. We have made sure that we save as many pictures as we can. We make sure we save pictures on our cell phones and other electronic devices.

One of the best things we enjoyed about Kaiden is that she attended school for a while until she got her trachea. She participated in the Christmas program at school with her classmates. We have some pictures of this. The school has always made crafts for her that can create memories for her.

Memories of Kaiden is all we will always have. We are creating some of the best memories now. Spending time with her every day and learning about her and who she is, I count it the biggest memory of all times. It is such a blessing to have Kaiden in our lives; she makes life so full and we are part of her memories too.

CHAPTER TEN

THINGS WILL HAPPEN BUT WE MUST ACCEPT IT AND DEAL WITH IT
[Kaiden Is In God's Hand]

Kaiden's health comes with a lot of complications. We really understand that there are a lot of issues that she faces day after day. There are times when there are loved ones that do not understand and the process gets really hard. Sometimes, we wonder if this is real and how can we overcome this. Sometimes, families in these situations feel alone. Our family has felt alone many days. Kaiden's mom and dad have had to face situations and not truly know what would happen to their daughter. They had to put their trust in the doctor's believing and hoping that things will turn out the way they should. Sometimes, people don't understand so they ask a lot of questions. This is truly understood, but the problem is that nobody has walked in our shoes. All they can do is tell us they love us all, and they are praying for Kaiden.

The pain that is felt when family members are trying to understand why Kaiden was born with so many issues, and the changes, makes the family nervous. I have watched the parents, aunt, uncle, and grandpa be so strong while caring for such a lovely child. These individuals are strong because in the midst of not knowing what will happen to Kaiden, they continue to stay strong. It is about always keeping hope and trusting that nothing else will come up. Kaiden has made amazing strides over the years. It is just when things happen to her, it is never small. So, when issues come up with her health and everything has been great over a span of time, and then something pops up, it is so scary for the family. There is always having to redirect our thoughts at all times so everything make sense. Kaiden is a child that has made a lot of adjustments and she doesn't complain by crying or being upset. If something bothers her, we have to read her body language, her body temperature, her pulse, and watch her seizure activity. The only time Kaiden cried tears is when she was in the hospital recently and she did not want to be intubated. She is a real trooper.

We have to basically live day by day, trusting and believing God that every day will be a good day for her. Some days are good and some days are bad. She has days when her body temperature drops to 92.1 and then we can only hope and pray that it will come back up, so we cover her up with blankets and warm the body and then we notice that when she gets warm, the pulse will begin to rise really fast and high. So then, we have to take the blankets off of her and cool her down. It is so hard sometimes, because you want to make sure that she does not have a septic infection. Once we took her to the doctor, she had no infection. It is just that her body does not have the ability to cool off and warm up like our body can. It is our job to know what she needs. She cannot say what she needs so we have to be alert for her twenty four hours, seven days a week.

As a family, we never complain about our time we get to spend with Kaiden. We enjoy taking care of her and we're glad she is a survivor. We have learned that we have to put Kaiden in the hands of the Lord. Her father and mother had a dedication service for her when she was two months old. They gave her back to God and I believe he is keeping Kaiden's body healed. There are times when she is feeling touch and go, but God is still moving in her life.

There is a feeling we have when we know deep in our heart that something is wrong. We feel fear. According to scripture, he says in Psalms 23:4, "Yea, though I walk through the valley of the death, I will fear no evil; for thou art with me, thy rod and thy staff they comfort me." Even though Kaiden has walked through the valley of death, we have constantly trusted God that we would not be afraid. He has helped us deal with her life.

I have learned that Kaiden is in the hands of the Lord and us going to God and talking to him, is the best thing we can do. So, we give Kaiden so much love so she can feel it.

Things happen and we have learned how to accept it and deal with it. It is scary at times; we wish things would change and even when they seem worse we go into prayer and to God in prayer about Kaiden and her parents and family. I watch, and things change drastically. I have seen God work miracles in her life. I have my times when I thought things were not going to get better, and they really did. So, it is important to believe that God can make things better for her, and he has.

We have learned to be there for Kaiden. We love her and we continue to speak good things over her. We are so grateful that she is still here with us and that she receives the care she needs.

CHAPTER ELEVEN

A GRANDMOTHER'S ROLE AND THE LOVE I HAVE FOR KAIDEN
[KAIDEN CHANGED MY LIFE]

It has been a privilege to grandparent such a sweet, loving, funny, and wonderful granddaughter. She means the world to me. Over eight years ago, when Kaiden was born, I was scared to get too close because of her diagnoses. I admit I did not want to be heartbroken. So, I expressed to her mom that I did not want to get close to her. Kaiden's mom looked me in the eye and said, "Mrs. Denise, hold Kaiden, it's okay to get close to her." I knew right then and there that I had a bond with her. Kaiden's mother and father allowed my husband and me to have a big role in her life. The attachment to Kaiden has been worth it all. Kaiden has been on assignment for years. She is the one that helped hold the family together for many years. Her very presence echoes who God really is in this world and how he works miracles. She has taught me love, forgiveness, patience, thankfulness, faith, hope, endurance, determination, joy, and to overcome. She has taught me how to truly love people.

When Kaiden was diagnosed, I was at the house heading to the hospital to see her. My husband called me and told me he needed me to be strong. I remember the day Kaiden's mom told her mother. When she and I went to the hospital to see her, she said to me, "Mrs. Denise, please take care of my granddaughter." We did discuss Kaiden's condition and how we were believing God that she would live longer than what the prognosis was. She surely did. To this day, I am living out what I promised my granddaughter's other grandmother (Ms. Francesca). She was a very sweet lady and her love for Kaiden is forever here.

I was expressing my level of fear concerning the possibility of Kaiden not living past three months. That was a hard pill to swallow. To be honest, I did know how to feel. This was my first granddaughter. I really began to feel like something evil had attacked my granddaughter. I was angry. I was focusing on the supernatural and what evil forces may have come to destroy her life. The day the doctors sent us home with Kaiden, they let us know she may not live past two months. In my mind, I said, God, how in the world did this happen to our grandchild? Why did this happen to my grandchild? I said, God, we all can't handle this. It is bigger than we are. It is too much to deal with and overcome. It will destroy us mentally and we will begin to give up. I was hurt really bad. I watched Kaiden's parents hurt, and it made me hurt. I watched some of Kaiden's aunts hurt, and it made me hurt. Our families where devastated. We never expected this to happen. I truly did not know how we would get through this. After leaving the hospital with Kaiden that day, we all went home and cried and I began to talk to God about my granddaughter. We began to fast and pray that God would give her a miracle and add years to her life. Kaiden taught me how to have faith in God. She taught me that just because the doctors gave the prognosis, it does not mean that things won't change. Things did change.

I have a motto about Kaiden. I never let her go to bed at night without praying for her. Once a week, I would have special prayer for her. Our faith in God is strong. Some people may say we have faith in a higher power. It is true God is my power; and he is a powerful God. He is omnipotent. That means that God is all powerful. God is amazing. He gave us a continual miracle. The day she came out of the hospital and lived past three months, that alone represented the miracle of God and from God.

I do realize that some people may not feel this strongly about what we have been through and the things we continue to face with Kaiden. I say that because they don't know our story, our struggles, and our fears. It has not been easy. Looking in from the outside, some people will never know the work we put in to keep our Kaiden at her best. She deserves the best. We go all out for her and it is a genuine love. A grandmother's love is a great thing. It is unselfish, very caring, and sacrificing when it comes to her. Some grandparents don't care, but we do. I am so elated to be in her life. But there has been times when I thought God had closed heaven to our prayers and didn't hear us and that he would not help us make it through. I learned that God doesn't look at us like man does. Man looks on the outside, but God looks at the heart. This was none of our faults; it just happened and we are taking care of her. She is the love of our lives and we can never be selfish, but enjoy her and let her know how important she is to us.

The love I have for Kaiden is undeniable and real. She is a big part of our family legacy. She is leaving a mark on this family, that cannot be erased. She is one of the biggest gifts that God has given us. She has been a blessing to everyone in the family. Her mother and father must always know that they gave us a beautiful child. Kaiden is so sweet. She is easy to take care of. All we have to do is show her love. She receives it and always smiles when she gets it.

Kaiden's smile has taught me not to frown. Anyone that knows us will tell you that all Kaiden does, is smile. Kaiden loves to hear other children talk and play. She smiles and responds by making cough sounds to let us know she hears us and we need to respond to her.

Kaiden is doing well. She likes to watch Paw Patrol, Dora, Doc Mc Stuffin, and Mickey Mouse club house; she hears their voices and is very stimulated by the sound. I love watching her as she listens to their voices. It lets me know that her brain is receiving some types of signals.

As I think about the role that I will have in Kaiden's life, I am so grateful, and what an opportunity to serve and be in my granddaughter's life. I am so thankful that her parents saw the love and heart that my husband and I have for Kaiden. I have been able to see her grow by leaps and bounds. The small things that she does are big in our eyes. I have a closeness to my granddaughter that is indescribable. I was so afraid to get close to her when she was first born. It is so good that I got close, because she changed my life.

It is my role to not only be a support to Kaiden, but I am her biggest advocate or voice. I know her parents have a voice too, but from a grandmother's perspective, I speak up for my granddaughter. I believe it is my responsibility to speak up on her behalf to those who provide services for her. I am not afraid to let them know that she has a personality and she has a way of letting us know how she feels about specific things. I am here to help protect her from danger, seen and unseen. I also pay attention to people that are around her and if they are sick, I have to respectfully protect her from sickness that is transferred from person to person. She has such a vulnerable immune system. We don't have a lot of people come to the house since she got the trachea, especially in the winter because so many people have had the flu.

It is my responsibility to pay attention to Kaiden and watch her body signals and learn when she is feeling good and when she is not. I always let her parents know when there is something different happening with her. She makes taking care of her so easy. This is why we take our time and see what she needs. It is my responsibility to be patient and I don't care how tired I am, I will get up and make sure she doesn't need changing and make sure she is not hungry. She has been such a big part of my life, I feel empty when she is not a round. Everything that I have to do for her I have learned it at warp speed because it is important that all her needs are met. We want her taken care of. I always make sure at night that she is sleeping ok. If her parents are around then I don't have to do that. I make sure her trachea and the equipment is working properly. If she looks sick, I call the doctors immediately. I know the warning signs so we have an emergency plan in place for her.

There is such a special bond between her and I. Nana's little angel, that is what she is to me. I wouldn't have had it any other way. I never thought that I would be able to pour so much love into one person. When she is afraid, I try to be the faith for her. She has a deepness to her soul. I feel when she looks into people's eyes, she looks into their soul. She can feel the spirit of a person. I feel she can tell if they are pure and genuine. I have seen her turn her head away from people that may sound a little mean. One day, I cried in front of her because my best friend died. My granddaughter found a way to lean into me. I feel she is so unique. She is God's little Sunshine. When I am close to her, I feel close to God. She has made me a better person.

My husband had me to come off my job when Kaiden was born because he wanted me to help out with her at home, and also because her parents were students in college. God provided a way for me to stay at home and care for her. I feel this is why she is so strong. All of us are her caregivers, and we have given her one on one attention, undistracted, with no excuses. We all will rearrange our life just to make sure we fit into her life. We are willing to make adjustments to do whatever is needed to make her stronger than she has ever been. She makes us so happy.

I remember when I had to have surgery and the doctors did not know whether or not I had cancer in my throat. I was somewhat afraid. God talked to me and he would let me know I was fine and he was with me. When I looked at my granddaughter and she would smile and make noises, it was almost like she was telling me, "Grandma, everything is going to be alright!" I always thought about the number of surgeries Kaiden had after she was born and how we saw the hand of God in her life. Then I would think that

I shouldn't even complain about my situation. Kaiden has been through more than most adults have and she wakes up from surgery smiling and laughing. This has helped me to understand that when I look at life to be bad, I have to remember how my granddaughter has survived a lot. She is a big survivor.

After my surgery was over, they did a biopsy on the growth they found in my throat and thank God, my doctor gave me a letter that said I had no cancer. All I could think about was that I stop complaining and begin to focus on the peace, joy, hope, and faith that God has given me over the years. Taking care of Kaiden has taught me how to be grateful and patient with the process that God helps us to get through. God has taken care of me. God knows I am one of my granddaughter's biggest caregivers and he is going to take care of me. I have learned that fear has no place in my life, only faith. Kaiden has caused me to walk in a level of faith that I never thought I would. She is so delicate, but yet so strong. When I look at her, I see God's strength and energy all in her body. I know that God has given me a high level of energy to take care of my granddaughter.

My role is to make her feel like she has the best life on earth. I want her to feel like a princess all the time. I can't stand to see her hurting or in pain. I will do all I can do to get that pain away from her. I make sure she dresses beautiful, smells beautiful, and feels beautiful. She is God's little Sunshine, but also God's little princess. It is my job to build her up and keep her strong for her parents. I make sure that she smiles.

I also take time and pray with her. He has taught me that instead of worrying about my granddaughter, to learn to pray for her, that God will intervene. I know some people don't believe in God and they have higher power. Well, God is my power source. I was put here to take care of my granddaughter, but I was also put here to pray for her. She is what keeps me in prayer a lot. I have learned to pray in the morning, noon, and night, and in between. I have learned to seek God for her when she doesn't feel good or when she is just simply having a hard day. I have learned to seek God for the smallest things in her life. Her life is filled with love and she has kept me believing and trusting in God. I have had to trust God every day for Kaiden to live. Even when she would get sick and we didn't know why, I trusted God for her. I have made a decision never to give up on what God can do for her.

Taking care of Kaiden helped me trust doctors. There was a time in my life where I lost faith in doctors because they made some mistakes with my care. I do understand that doctors are not perfect and they do try the best they can. They have done a good job with my granddaughter's care. I realize that her case has not been easy and we have had to work as a team with them to keep them up on her health. They have tried their best to make her life as comfortable as it can be.

Kaiden taught me to live life to the fullest and enjoy my time with her. I used to focus on the wrong things. I would sit around and worry about Kaiden, and this was not helping a thing. Then, when I would look at her in the face, I could see her saying, Nana, you need to smile more and stop worrying about me. I am going to be fine. Things are not really that bad. I can remember hoping that her life would be comfortable for her. She deserves to be comfortable. She was diagnosed with so many illnesses. We have made a choice to do all we can to make her life successful. I am not going to be afraid, because she is in the hands of God. I have learned to do what I need to do for Kaiden and not worry what anyone thinks. I had a woman say to me one time that she would not be willing to take care of her grandchild like I do. She felt that was too much work. She said she did not sign on for all of what I am doing. I immediately responded by letting her know that those are her feelings, not mine. I let her know that she has a right to feel the way she chooses, but please don't put her convictions off on me about my granddaughter. This is my grandchild and God blessed our family with her. I chose not to be friends with that lady. I love Kaiden and I do not worry about the care I give her. I feel I want to give her the best love and care a Nana can give. I don't regret the way I have taken care of her over the years. I just want to continue to be there for her as long as I can. I love her and I want the best for my granddaughter. I keep negative vibes away from her. She is one of the strongest. I believe a positive atmosphere will create a positive person. My role in Kaiden's life is to keep her strong and keep negative people and negative words away from her. I plan to continue to love her and always let her know every day of her life that she is very important to us.

Kaiden doesn't require a lot. Kaiden receives nursing care. We always pick nurses that are positive and truly want to work with children. We look at the nursing staff as being one of the main caregivers. Kaiden spends a lot of time with them throughout her day. Not only do we look at them as her nurses, but we treat them like family. All Kaiden knows, is family, and she loves everyone the same. Kaiden is very stimulated by family, friends, nurses, and other health care professionals talking to her. We have a good home healthcare agency and they always send good nurses to work with Kaiden. We are grateful to have such good people helping us to get Kaiden strong and back the way she used to be.

One thing that worried me for a long time was that we applied for so many life insurances and no companies in the United States will give us a life insurance policy for her because of her prognosis we received from when she was a child. So, we made a decision to just put money away and if something comes up we will do what we have to do to make sure she is taken care of. We have faced some hard information about Kaiden and then we had to learn to deal with it. My heart goes out to her mom and dad, so instead of worrying about it, I wanted them to know that we will help take care of her if that situation arises.

Over the years, taking care of my granddaughter has helped me realize that she has a story. Her mere existence for all these years is a story in itself. Kaiden needs to let the world know that she is still here because of God, but also she is a fighter. Kaiden means warrior and she is always ready to fight when the wars come in her life. She has been through many storms and she is still smiling. I have watched Kaiden have seizures all day. But even when Kaiden doesn't feel her best, she acts like she is feeling so good. I asked God to teach me how to have Kaiden's attitude and peaceful disposition.

I have begun to realize that God doesn't want me worrying about Kaiden, but he wants me enjoying my time with her and building good memories and encouraging her parents. If I focus on the good things about Kaiden's life and stop worrying about the future and what could happen to her, then I will be able to truly enjoy her.

I realized over the years that Kaiden has learned a lot. She may not have been able to keep it all in her memory, but she is holding on to what she has already learned. Getting her education has been very important for her. She learned how to socialize at school. We always wanted to make sure that she had an EIP to follow for her class. I have met with the principal teacher, school nurse, occupational therapist, physical therapist, music teacher, gym teacher, and the school for the blind. I was able to connect with them and we have been able to make a good connection with the school. We want her strong so she can go to school once again; but because of her health, she has to be taught at home.

God has a plan for Kaiden. I may not always see it but I realize God is putting everything in her life the way he wants it to be. God has plans for the world to see her strength and how Kaiden responds. I would love to see Kaiden interact with others more. As soon as she can get really strong and be around other children, then social characteristics will kick in again. We can always tell if she is overwhelmed by that day or has had too much stimulation.

Spending time with her makes me feel good. She lights up our house. She has been the glue that holds our family together. There are no regrets. We only have love for this little girl. She is God's little Sunshine and she is definitely just that.

I even enjoy shopping for Kaiden. It has been so much fun. I try to buy her things that will be suitable for a little girl. I try to get clothes I know her parents would like too. I also try to buy her clothes at least once a month. I make sure she is always stocked with shirts, socks, tee-shirts, pants, shorts, dresses, jeans, and whatever she needs. I want to make sure she is stocked up and we don't have to worry about anything. I have purchased plenty of clothes and once they are too small, we share them with others in our community.

Kaiden is even loved by people that have never met her. She has so many people that love her. When she was in the hospital, people that didn't know her sent up prayers and came by to see her.

She is definitely God's little Sunshine. She has a glow and God has put life in her. She is God's little girl and he does know what is best for her. God wants the parents, grandparents, great grandparents, aunts, uncles, cousins, and longtime friends to stay encouraged and to keep encouraging Kaiden to be strong and just show her how God loves every time you see her.

God created Kaiden, and even when it seems she doesn't feel her best, we must keep the faith and keep encouraging her that she will make it. I just want her to feel good about herself. I want us to keep speaking positive over her life. I want us to love her and remind her of how important she is to God. She is very important to God and he doesn't make any mistakes. She is not a mistake, she is a miracle that God is using in this world to show people that God still works miracles. Miracles are sometimes not expected to happen. But God has created a miracle for Kaiden and that is to live life and for this, we are so grateful.

I am truly holding onto my purpose in my granddaughter's life and I am happy that God let me be here to help her. I will always love and cherish Kaiden Enjoli Upchurch.

This journey with Kaiden in my life is teaching me so much. I am so excited about the other grandchildren that God is going to give me. I will always give my best to them and Kaiden. I can't wait to the day that I will be able to say that I helped my granddaughter experience good things.

We have taught Kaiden what love is. She has always felt our love and she continues to feel it now. We talk to Kaiden all the time. She has family, nurses, teachers, and health care providers that spend time loving her. When the providers, nurses, and educators come into the home, I remind them that this house has a family feel to it. So, when people come in, Kaiden feels that family touch with everyone. Kaiden is that type of child who if myself and papa don't spend our grandparents' time with her, she will get mad. I feel that as her grandparents, we should always be in her corner. We feel that Kaiden deserves the best. There is always something we can give her or do better with her. As her grandparents, we want to give her what she seems to like. She is the type of child who when you dress her up, do her hair, and put jewelry on her, she will smile. She knows she looks good and there is nothing that anyone can do about it. We tell her every day that she is beautiful and special to us. She loves a lot of hugs. We hug her every day and remind her that we are so glad she is here. Kaiden will smile and stretch her eyes as to say, I love my Nana and Papa. We have a special place in her life and we are so glad God let us be a part of it.

Kaiden is so in tune that she can tell when someone new is in the house. As her Nana, I taught her how to be informed. I ask everyone new that comes to talk to her just like they would anyone else. She has a way of listening and looking. Kaiden may have been diagnosed with some issues, but this little can discern her surroundings. She watches, looks and even make faces when something is not right. She is the type of child that will get quiet and won't say much. Once the person opens their mouth and speaks to her, then she will respond in her own way.

I have always sang with Kaiden. She loves music. I always felt it was Nana's joy to sing to her. Then sometimes, I would let her come in the kitchen while I cook and I would talk to her. I would explain to her how I made my sweet potatoes pies. There was one time I allowed her to put her hand in my sweet potato mix so she could feel the texture of the potatoes. I would also let her know when I was making biscuits, pancakes, or even cookies. I remember one time, I let her hold the spoon while I supported her hand and helped her stir it. She really liked that. I felt that these were moments that grandparents share with their grandchild and not miss out on this opportunity to educate her. She really enjoys spending time with Nana and Papa, we have a different style from that of Mom and Dad.

Kaiden is everything I expected her to be, and more. She is the sweetest and smartest little girl I know. She may not be able to understand as much as other children but what excites me is that she understands something. She is my shining star.

I prayed so hard for her during her battle with pneumonia. I feel that was a big part of Nana's role in her life. I always pray for Kaiden every day. I always speak over her life and say positive things. I feel she has survived this long because of God and because of the love of all her caregivers. She is God's little Sunshine. She is always smiling and making other people feel good. I love the way she never frowns. Kaiden wakes up smiling. She is a happy little girl. My role is to keep her happy. I keep encouraging her by loving her and letting her know, every day, she was meant to be here and that she is important. I am so grateful for this opportunity. I always show Kaiden what it is to respect and treat other people right. I always let her hear honesty, integrity, and truthfulness in my voice. Kaiden knows the spirit of every person in this house. She knows our real side. She is not a child that doesn't pay attention, she does. She understands more than what some professionals may realize. She knows when her mom, dad, nana, papa, auntie, and uncle walk into the house and speak. It is so real for her and I can tell she loves being included and talked too. We always remember her all the time. All year around, she is celebrated. Every day, it is important to our family that she lives. She is such an inspiration to us all. She has an amazing assignment of encouraging us all to stay on the right track. Kaiden has already secured her seat in Heaven. We just got to keep doing what's right to make it in with her. She is like a precious stone. She is pure and shines with a big gleam. She is God's little Sunshine. She is shining when no one sees her. Her life is shining.

She stands up big in the world. She is an example to families that want to give up. She keeps giving and giving. This is why we love her so much. I count it a great opportunity to serve as her grandmother. She is a wonderful child to take care of and she has been a joy for me and helped me through the hard times in my life. Taking care of Kaiden has taught me what a grandmother's role really is. I am a big advocate for her and I will always give her all the love I have. I am glad to have shared my life with her and I will always remember this the rest of my life. She is part of the family's legacy. She is a representation of God's glory on the earth. She represents the fact that God still works miracles. She is God's little Sunshine.

Writing this book about my granddaughter and the care we have given her has been a blessing. I have seen her life from every angle possible. I have learned about Kaiden's brain abnormality. I have learned about her other twelve diagnoses. She is a blessing to have in our lives. She is such a sweet little lady. She is a joy to care for. She is my inspiration. She means the world to us. So, as you have read this book, I truly hope that it has been a blessing to you and those who read it. Kaiden's life is an example to many. I hope this encourages families that feel their loved one may not survive. I have two quick suggestions and they are 1, don't allow people to discourage you; don't tell them everything, and 2, Love and love and love some more. Children with these types of issues can really survive and be very optimistic, and if you are religious, "Trust in God!"

I do realize that she is God's little Sunshine and God has done amazing work on her. So, realize that the same blessings that came upon my granddaughter can happen with someone else.

CHAPTER TWELVE

MY AFFIRMATION, MY FAITH IN GOD, AND MY MIRACLE
[God Did It!]

This is so amazing that I was able to share with the world how precious my granddaughter is to me. I have a love that no one can take from a grandmother. I have an opportunity that I will always remember and never regret. I can never put a price on the love that we share. I am grateful for every second that I have been able to share with my granddaughter. She is God's little Sunshine. She has brought our family so much love and hope that I am changed forever.

I realize that everyone does not share the same religious belief nor experiences. I realize that some people believe in a higher power. I do believe in a higher power and for me, it is God. During this journey with my granddaughter, God has been my source of strength, my confidant, my friend, my hope, my peace, and even my joy. God has been my faith and my total belief system. I have had to trust God for my granddaughter's life, her father and mother's strength, and our family's dream that Kaiden will continue to be in our lives for as long as God will allow her to. Our family has had to trust God for Kaiden's total existence. It has been a one day at a time process.

The fact that Kaiden is here, it proves that there is a God. The fact that she is alive and still living with no frontal lobe (brain), pinpoints to me that there is a God. This is a miracle and God is at the top of it. Kaiden was supposed to have not lived past three months. She is eight years old. I believe God and no one will ever convince me that God is not real. God is real.

This was a challenge and we began to pray right after she was born and made the decision that we would trust God for Kaiden's very life. We came together and cried and prayed unto God. I believe God heard our cry. We realized that from the beginning, it would take the supernatural power of God to get us through this ordeal with Kaiden. We were in need of God's love, peace, hope, comfort, and even joy for when the hard times come. We were distraught at the beginning of her life, but eight years later, we have seen the hands of God. Our faith in God and his Word is what has made us all who we are today. All of our lives have been changed and we believe God now more than ever.

All of Kaiden's doctors have been phenomenal. I consider them the handiwork of God. He has used them to help her and create the best plan of care for her. We have made some lasting relationships and even created new friendships that cannot be broken. One thing I can say about Kaiden's doctors is that they know she is a miracle. She has defied all of what should have happened to her. God was at the helm of the ship of her life and he was leading us all in what direction to take Kaiden in and the safest way to get her to where she has to go. Even through a host of surgeries, clinic visits, being in the pediatric intensive care unit for almost two months, and all the medical care, God was still right there.

I always believed from the beginning that God always had an angel around Kaiden. She was always protected by God's ministering angels. I believe wherever she went, the angel that was assigned to her was there, and the angel is still there right now. There was an Angel on assignment for my granddaughter, Kaiden Enjoli Upchurch. I am so grateful for that.

I will say this journey has not been a cake walk for us, but it has been a faith walk. Nothing else would work, but only our faith in God. God intervened and he has given us strength to continue to be the support that Kaiden needs in her life. We had to put Kaiden in the hands of God and let him do the work he wanted to do. We were helpless there was nothing that even the doctors could do sometimes, but God showed up and made everything ok.

It is always pleasurable to tell the world about how she has overcame so many obstacles. Watching her struggle and yet, smile, lets me know that God is with her. Kaiden has had many struggles, but she has also had many successes. This book has brought back so many memories of how she first began this journey of life. I felt pain while writing the book, but writing has helped me overcome the pain. I did receive healing by writing this book. I know that God has seen us through and he will continue to make it.

The solace we have had in our life is God, the prayers, the support of church family, friends, and an array of people that adore our little Sunshine. One of the major things that kept me going has been my time of meditation on God's Word, prayer, reading inspirational books, watching inspirational movies, and even spending time with people that inspire and build me up. My mom, and my aunt, Judy, were good for calling our family and letting us know that Kaiden would be fine, just keep praying and trusting God. We have done just what they told us to do and it really worked. Because of such amazing encouragement from so many, God has given us amazing strength. When Kaiden's situation would get bad, I would meditate on God's word; and then when it would get better, I would give him praise for what God had done for us all.

In this part of the book, I am sharing my transparency because I feel it may help someone know that all of us have to make changes in our life. We are not perfect and we don't have to look for acceptance from anyone. As long as God accepts me for who I am, that's all that really matters to me. During this time, I needed God to change my mindset about how I viewed life. God did it. Kaiden's situation made me a better person and gave me a better way of seeing life. I am a very positive person now. I learned that when I began to focus on Kaiden's situation and stopped worrying about myself, things changed for me. I learned how to be unselfish. I have learned how to love unconditionally. I believe that we just don't haphazardly go through things in life. Everything we go through in this life could possibly be for a reason. I prayed for years and asked God to change me and make me a better person and who he wanted me to be. God did just that. He did it through my granddaughter. Make no mistake, it has not felt good because I learned that my life belongs to God, and not myself. There are times that I felt angry because of my granddaughter's situation. But the still small voice of God let me know that you all can handle this. You can bear this. I know it hurts. God let me know that Kaiden needed her parents, grandparents, great-grandparents, uncles, aunties, and all her family and friends to be strong for her and believe that she will come out on top! Kaiden's nurses, doctors, and other health care professionals have all been positive when it comes to her, and seeing that let me know that God wanted me to know that being positive has helped Kaiden fight to live and be around all these great people.

I want to share with you the way that I coped with my granddaughter's situation. I feel it may help those of you that are in this situation or similar situations.

Antoinette's Way of Coping

- First, I would always go off to a quiet place and get by myself. I would get still and quiet. I would cut my cell phone off and let my family know I wanted to spend some time alone. I would sit on the floor; or you may want to sit in a chair. I would cross my legs in an Indian style. I would lean my head toward the center of my lap and take five deep breaths. This was preparation for me to begin my meditation.

- Secondly, I would begin to empty my mind from all my cares and this process would take me at least ten minutes. Once my mind was empty, I would picture myself in a place that I always wanted to go. In my place, I pictured myself in the most beautiful part of Africa where the water is so beautiful. I would envision the sun beating down on my face and I could hear the waterfalls all around me, and I could hear the wind blowing in the air.

- Thirdly, I would then begin to pray and tell God how I was feeling inside. I admit, I was crying and felt angry because I was feeling my granddaughter did not deserve to be born like this. I was angry because I wanted to be able to buy my granddaughter a bike and watch her ride it. I was angry because she could not talk to me and say Nana. I was angry because I wanted to be able to see her walk around and play with my new grandchildren that will come in the future. I told God I was angry and that I needed to feel his love. I always felt a warm touch go over my body. Immediately, God reminded me that most children with Kaiden's diagnoses don't even live this long. He reminded me of how Kaiden knows who we are. He reminded me how Kaiden will try to communicate and show love to her family. He reminded me that she was still alive. I began to be so thankful. So, this was a time of crying and releasing my feelings unto God and just being transparent about my granddaughter's life. I began to feel much better. Note: Crying is always a good way of releasing your feelings. I was being honest with myself and with God. I know God could feel my hurt and pain and he does love me.

- The fourth thing I would do would be to thank God for taking care of Kaiden thus far. I found myself so grateful for such a miracle. Then I would pray about things she was going through in her health. I would ask God to touch her body and give her strength. I also would ask God to give her peace and make her as comfortable as possible. I would even ask him to continue to heal her and let his love shine upon her. I could tell Kaiden heard me praying. I would see her smile and she would even find a way to make a little sound to let me know she heard me. That made me feel so good. After I prayed to God for about an hour, I would ask God to help me keep a strong mindset and remain positive. I wanted God to help me be that example to and for my family. I would always end the prayer and say thank you God for another day that Kaiden has lived. I would hold Kaiden in my lap and she has a way of pulling herself close to you. That alone made me feel so good. I would always feel the love of God in the room when I would pray, and that let me know he was there with me.

- The fifth and final thing I would do is read my Bible. Reading the Bible not only gave me hope and inspiration, but it gave me power and faith to believe what God has said. During my period of coping, meditation on the Word of God made me so strong mentally, emotionally, and spiritually.

I want to share my scriptures, my affirmations, and quotes that have helped me stay grounded in my granddaughter's life.

Scriptures that help with encouragement:

> *Psalms 31:24*—Be strong and take heart, all you who hope in the Lord.
>
> *Psalms 16:8*—I keep my eyes always on the Lord. With him at my right hand, I will not be shaken.
>
> *1 Peter 5:7*—Cast all your anxiety on him because he cares for you.
>
> *Psalms 120:1*—I call on the Lord in my distress, and he answers me.

Scriptures that gave me hope:

> *Job 6:8*—Oh, that I might have my request, that God would grant what I hope for.

Proverbs 13:12—Hope deferred makes the heart sick, but a longing fulfilled is a tree of life.

Scriptures that gave me peace:

Philippians 4:6–7—Do not be anxious about anything, but in every situation, by prayer and petition, with thanksgiving, present your requests to God. And the peace of God, which transcends all understanding, will guard your hearts and minds through Christ Jesus.

Jeremiah 29:11—The Lord gives strength to his people; the Lord blesses his people with peace.

Scriptures that brought encouragement about Kaiden being healed:

Psalms 34:20—For the Lord will sustain him upon his sick bed; in his illness, you restore him to health.

Proverbs 16:24—Gracious words are like a honeycomb, sweetness to the soul and health to the body.

Jeremiah 17:14—Heal me, O Lord, and I shall be healed; save me and I shall be saved, for you are my praise.

Scriptures about how God loves us:

Psalms 136:26—Give thanks to the God of Heaven, for his steadfast love endures forever.

Chronicles 16:34—Give thanks to the Lord, for He is good; his love endures forever.

Isaiah 43:2—When you pass through the waters, I will be with you; and through the rivers, they shall not overflow you. When you walk through fire (hard times in life), you shall not be burned; nor shall the flame scorch you.

These are the scriptures I meditated upon, and they gave me great comfort and strength.

My Daily Affirmations

I used these affirmation to affirm my hope and what I truly believe in. I affirmed them because they kept me strong and focused. I am glad to have created these affirmations; they helped me so much.

My Affirmations

- I will not give up!
- I will believe that things will change and get better!
- I will keep a positive mindset no matter what the day may bring!
- I am an overcomer!
- This situation will not make me lose hope!
- It doesn't matter where I start, only where I finish!
- God is bigger than my situation!
- I have God's love and my granddaughter will make it through!
- I am a winner; and I win in every situation!
- I will make lemonade out of the lemons life has handed me!
- I am a product of hope!
- I will not let people's words or opinions bring me down!
- I will stay strong!
- I will love every day, and not hate!
- I will forgive all that has hurt me so I can remain healed!
- I will always believe the best for my granddaughter!
- My granddaughter will receive a miracle today!
- I am a miracle!
- My family is a miracle!
- Today is the best day of the rest of our lives!

Daily Quotes that Lifted my Spirit

> Martin Luther King—"But I know, somehow, that only when its dark enough can you see the stars."
>
> Alfred Tennyson—"Smiles from the threshold of the years to come, whispering it will be happier…"
>
> Barbara Kingsolver—"The very least you can do in your life is figure what you hope for. And the most you can do is live inside that hope, not admire it from a distance but live right in it, under its roof."
>
> Pablo Nervda—"You can cut all the flowers but you cannot keep spring from coming."
>
> Anne Frank, The Diary of a Young Girl—"I don't think of all the misery, but of the beauty that still remains."
>
> Cecelia Ahern—"Shoot for the moon, even if you fall, you'll land among stars."
>
> Carl Sandburg—"A baby is God's opinion that the world should go on."
>
> Roy T. Bennett—"Never lose hope. Storms make people stronger and never last forever."

This is a great opportunity to share my journey with my granddaughter, with the world. I hope this book touches the hearts of those who may be encountering some struggles as I am. I want you to know that you can survive. In your weakest moment, you will recognize the strength you have within.

MEET KAIDEN

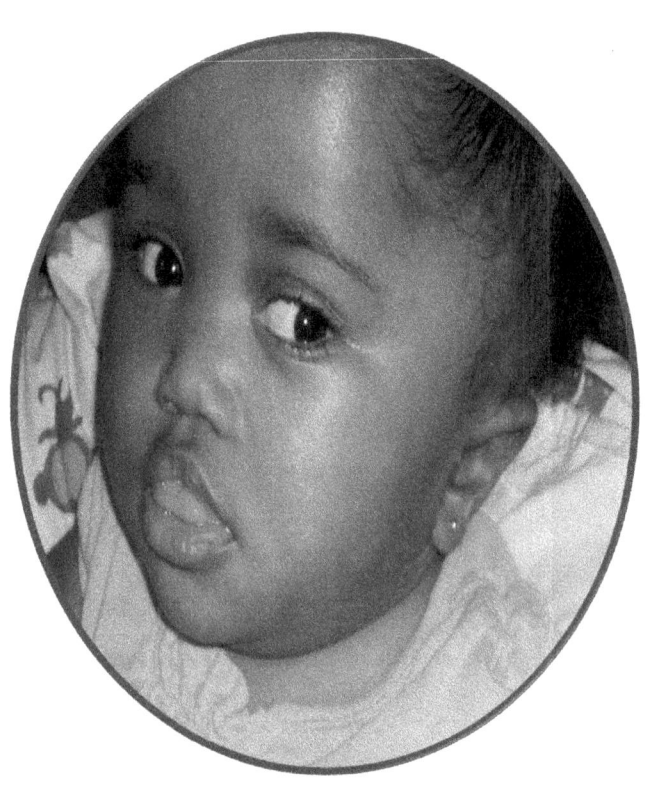

ABOUT THE AUTHOR
ANTOINETTE D. UPCHURCH

Biography of Senior Pastor Antoinette Denise Upchurch

Senior Pastor Antoinette Upchurch is a native of Sanford, NC and is a God-fearing woman that fell in love with Jesus at the tender age of 8 years old; and through the years she has developed a powerful relationship with the Lord!

Senior Pastor Antoinette Upchurch has been married to Bishop Ulysses Upchurch for 28years; and they have 3 wonderful children and one beautiful granddaughter that she gladly takes care of.

Senior Pastor Antoinette Upchurch received her spiritual foundation as a youth an adult under Bishop Charles Mellette of Christian Provision Ministries, Sanford, NC and Bishop Jerry Brown out of Virginia Beach, Virginia, during her husband's time in the United States Navy.

Senior Pastor Antoinette Upchurch pastors alongside her husband Bishop Ulysses Upchurch. They established Increasing Faith Deliverance Ministries of Sanford 14 years ago. She became Senior Pastor of Increasing Faith Deliverance Ministries in July of 2014. She also assists her husband with the Increasing Faith Affiliate of Ministries Fellowship. Also in the past she served as Associate Pastor for two years, and Youth Pastor for five years at her former churches. She has preached throughout the Eastern Coast of the United States and took missions trips overseas. She and her husband are now serving under the Spiritual Covering of Bishop Charles Mellette out of Sanford, NC.

Senior Pastor Antoinette Upchurch received her formal education through Bryant and Stratton College, Virginia Beach, Va., earning an Associate Degree in Medical Office Management. She earned a Bachelor's Degree in Biblical Studies from Bethel Seminary College, Sanford, NC. She also obtained her Bachelor's Degree in Counseling with an Emphasis on Substance Abuse, from Grand Canyon University Online in December, 2015. She is presently attending Grand Canyon University On-line located in Phoenix, Arizona. She is expected to receive her Master's in Addiction Counseling in January, 2019.

Senior Pastor Antoinette Upchurch is always excited about preaching and teaching the gospel and encouraging all people that God has ordained a better life for them.

www.ingramcontent.com/pod-product-compliance
Lightning Source LLC
Chambersburg PA
CBHW071621040426
42452CB00009B/1428